My Spiritual Journey

LIFE AS AN EMPATH

Jacinta Yang

BALBOA.PRESS

A DIVISION OF HAY HOUSE

Balboa Press books may be ordered through booksellers or by contacting:

Balboa Press
A Division of Hay House
1663 Liberty Drive
Bloomington, IN 47403
www.balboapress.com
844-682-1282

Because of the dynamic nature of the Internet, any web addresses or
links contained in this book may have changed since publication and
may no longer be valid. The views expressed in this work are solely those
of the author and do not necessarily reflect the views of the publisher,
and the publisher hereby disclaims any responsibility for them.

The author of this book does not dispense medical advice or prescribe the use
of any technique as a form of treatment for physical, emotional, or medical
problems without the advice of a physician, either directly or indirectly. The
intent of the author is only to offer information of a general nature to help
you in your quest for emotional and spiritual well-being. In the event you use
any of the information in this book for yourself, which is your constitutional
right, the author and the publisher assume no responsibility for your actions.

Any people depicted in stock imagery provided by Getty Images are
models, and such images are being used for illustrative purposes only.
Certain stock imagery © Getty Images.

Print information available on the last page.

ISBN: 978-1-9822-6490-1 (sc)
ISBN: 978-1-9822-6492-5 (hc)
ISBN: 978-1-9822-6491-8 (e)

Library of Congress Control Number: 2021903914

Balboa Press rev. date: 03/16/2021

Contents

I dedicate this book to Krista Tucci, who is a very dear and special friend. We felt an instant comfort like home when we first met. She is a soul sister who came into my life at the most perfect time and helped me through the process of having my first book published. Krista, you have been so kind and patient and generous with your time. Thank you for offering to be there to help me to overcome the technical difficulties I may encounter in order to publish my upcoming books. I feel we are now on our spiritual journey together and look forward to seeing where our path leads us. I am so happy and grateful to have such a beautiful soul with me during my journey.

Acknowledgements

I am grateful to everyone who has crossed my path. Without them I would not be who I am today. Many have had positive impacts on my life.

I want to acknowledge the late Sister Elfreda D'souza, who had a great impact on my spiritual journey. Her life as a nun influenced me to dedicate my life to helping others. When my family arranged my marriage, she wrote to me, "Jacinta, God has other plans for you. You may not be a nun, but you can still help people as you have always wanted." Those words meant a lot to me, and she was right. I can still help others without being a nun, and that is what I have done and continue to do.

I am thankful for having my son in my life, who was the main reason that led me on the journey to reclaim my life. In the quest to do so it led me on the journey to go within to find the strength I had. I learnt a lot more about me, my strengths and all the gifts I possess to be the person I am today.

I am grateful to my siblings, all older than me, as they have been great examples of love, patience, kindness, and generosity.

Special thanks to Brian Darwen for being that special friend I have known for more than two decades. As you have always said to me, true friends can be counted on your fingers, and you are one of them. Just as the saying goes, "A friend in need is a friend indeed." You certainly have been that friend. You have always had faith and believed in me in all that I do. You always supported me over the years, both personally and professionally, and are someone I can always count on. There are no words that can describe my gratitude.

Thanks to Hester for being a great support in the journey I am currently on and for trusting and acknowledging my gifts and ability to help those who can benefit from my healing gifts and guidance.

I am grateful to so many of my clients for having trust in me to help them on their healing journeys—Anne-Marie Henzel, Krista Tucci, Ashanti Dissanayake, Julia Pandolfo, Santha (also your daughter Annabelle), and Emily Lai to name a few. Without your commitments and efforts on your parts, it would not have been possible for me to know that I can make a difference.

Chapter 1

Spirituality

What Is Spirituality?

What is spirituality? I am sure many of you have asked this question
at some time or another, just as I have. In my teenage years and early
twenties, I really hadn't heard of it. Or rather, if I had, I was not
aware of it, or it had not caught my attention.

I would say I was in my late twenties the first time it caught my
attention. I was with a neighbour from the condominium I was living
in with whom I played squash. During one of our conversations, I
may have mentioned I was Catholic, and he told me he did not
follow any religion but was very spiritual.

I did not think too much of it at the time, but the word "spiritual"
certainly did stick in my head. I thought being spiritual was a good
thing, but I really did not quite comprehend the meaning of the
word.

Many have written about what spirituality is. Different people have
different views or concepts of spirituality. I feel that people need to
understand what it means for them on their terms based on their
personal journeys in life.

You can learn more about spirituality from information available on this topic and from others who have their own stories to tell. I believe spirituality is flexibility, openness, compassion, and unconditional love, and our individual understandings of spirituality are based on our own personal journeys toward our divine. This type of spirituality is different from spirituality based on religion, which is more community based and follows a certain set of rules and regulations constructed by someone else who seemed to have some wisdom.

Spiritual practices based on religion place more emphasis on knowledge and community, with the goal of salvation. To me, spirituality is more about openness to love and compassion and the freedom of personal growth. Spirituality emphasizes the wisdom of our journeys to our divine sources. Spirituality is a broad concept that is open to various perspectives, leaving room for personal growth and the search for the meaning of life that resonates with you personally.

It also relates to the essence of a person's spirit, inner being, soul, or inner self. For some, spirituality is about the essence of our souls or spirits that carries on beyond our physical lives, hence the saying, "We are spiritual beings having a human experience." When we complete our physical lives here, our souls or spirits live on. There is this belief that we come back again and again, having different lifetimes.

For others, spirituality is about having a sense or feeling of knowing that there is something greater than ourselves as human beings. It is a sense of connection to something bigger.

I noticed that the words "spiritual" and "spirituality" have become common buzzwords over the past fifteen or more years. I think this is because more and more people are trying to get in touch with themselves every day, going inward and doing soul-searching. For some, they are trying to see beyond the surface and materialistic life.

If you are reading this book, you are probably doing some soul-searching and seeking answers as to what your life is all about and where it will lead you. You may be wondering, or have wondered, about your purpose in life. There is so much to understand about yourself and why you are here on earth. There is so much to take in and digest about life and its meaning.

You may feel there is so much you need to learn and want to learn. You may have some spiritual gifts that you have just started to realize. You may even have experienced some drastic and life-changing experiences that led you to this quest to understand more about spirituality. I would say, we are about to start our spiritual journeys on a conscious level.

Understanding Spirituality

The word "spirituality" has been stuck in my head since my neighbour told me that he was spiritual rather than religious. I think there is a reason for it. Twenty-plus years later, I feel that may have been my pivot towards trying to understand spirituality. However, the journey was initially slow and gradual. Then one day I stumbled upon a sign in a storefront close to the flower shop I worked at, at the time. The sign read, "Church of Spiritual Wisdom." It piqued my curiosity, and I wondered, *Hmmm … I wonder what this is?* I remembered what my neighbour said about being spiritual. I proceeded to read the flyer on the window, checking the schedule for their meditation and spiritual circle. I was curious to learn more about what it meant to be spiritual.

When I look back, I think that was the start of my spiritual journey, even though I didn't know I was going into one, as some people actually do. I didn't decide, *Yeah, this is something I am interested in.* I think it was more like I had the spiritual gifts but was not really aware of them, or it was meant for me to go on this path. I wasn't really on it consciously. Nor had I made a decision to go on this path. Instead, it was like I was being led to it.

Before then, I had been invited to go on this journey on many occasions. I had many spiritual experiences, even though I did not pay too much attention to them or make too much fuss over them. I simply shrugged them off as experiences I had or signs that I had a very good imagination.

At a young age I had been very spiritual, but I did not know it. I guess you could say my spiritual journey back then was more of a religious kind, which I will talk about later. As a child, I had always been drawn to the spiritual way of living. I was always interested in wanting to help others. I was always compassionate, though I did not realize that I was an empath as well. Being compassionate is one of the traits of an empath.

There was so much about this journey that I didn't pay much attention to because I was too busy dealing with my daily life struggles; I wrote about these in my previous book, *Take Charge*. I was on my life's journey and my spiritual journey simultaneously. But back then it was more important for me to focus on surviving and overcoming my life's challenges than to try to understand what spirituality was all about.

During this life journey I had many spiritual experiences that were really incredible. Yet I didn't put too much weight on them or dwell on them, as at the time, I needed to stay focused on what I needed to do with my daily life. I was more focused in finding myself. Come to think of it, the spiritual side of me may have motivated my desire to grow and improve my very being.

I would say the spiritual gifts that I had have helped me in my life's journey that led me to where I am today. Because of my very strong logical nature and the multiple challenges I faced in earlier phases of my life, I simply had no time to consider trying to understand my spiritual side.

I think the logical side of me kept me from understanding more about spirituality for a fair number of years. I now know that if we are meant to be on a spiritual path or do spiritual work, we will find our ways to the path—be it intentionally or unintentionally—no matter how much we want to avoid it.

Due to my many spiritual experiences, I continued to seek to understand more about spirituality. This led me to spiritualist churches, which were more about life after death. I attended their spiritual developmental circles and realized that I had the gift of connecting to the spiritual realm. I have on various occasions connected to the spirit realm but always shrugged it off as the product of an active imagination as I am by nature a very creative person.

I shall get into my various spiritual experiences that are related to spirits or the afterlife later.

Types of Spirituality

I did not realize that there were different types of spirituality until I decided to gain a better understanding of spirituality. Through my research on spirituality, I have come to understand that there is a difference between spirituality and spiritualism. Since the words are so similar, they can be mistaken to be one and the same. There are so many articles written about spirituality, so I won't go into much detail on this subject. I will just outline a few simple concepts before taking you on my spiritual journey.

When we speak of types of spirituality or spiritualism, basically it is more about the spiritual practices that people follow, such as religious practices like Christianity, Buddhism, yoga, shamanism, meditations, and so on. There is plenty of information available out there if you would like more in-depth and detailed knowledge on the concept of spirituality.

Here I give you a brief introduction on a few types of spirituality. The types of spirituality are categorized as follows:

> *Heart-based spirituality* is a connection to the divine through the heart by prayer, devotion, gratitude, and unconditional love.

> *Metaphysical spirituality* is connected through the nonmaterial realm, such as energy healing (reiki), divination, channelling, astrology, and spirit guides.

> *Earth-based spirituality* is connecting through the earth and material realms, like healing with herbs or crystals.

> *Body-based spirituality* is connecting to the divine through breath work, meditation, channelling, chanting, and dancing.

For me, spirituality is a way of life. It is all about trying to connect to the divine or our true selves by living lives of compassion, awareness, integrity, and honesty.

Spirituality vs Religion

To differentiate between spirituality and religion is not exactly an easy task. I say this because I feel it is not all that easy for me to express my thoughts clearly or with ease. However, I shall attempt to explain it as best as I can so as not to make it too confusing.

Religion, for me, is something that was formulated by people who were considered wise and had a connection to the divine. These people are what most consider prophets, followers, or disciples of these prophets. I believe some rules, regulations, or rituals were formulated for people to live by.

Over time, different religions came into existence through changes made by prophets. In some cases, a new division of religion was born because a king decided he wanted to make some changes to suit himself. That is why there are various extensions of Christianity.

Religion has rules, regulations, and rituals for people to live by or follow in their lives in the Bible, the Koran, and other books written with teachings about God or the divine. Even though there are differences amongst these religions, the Koran and the Bible have the same stories from the time of Adam. The Old Testament and the earlier portion of the Koran contain the same stories.

The difference is notable in the New Testament for Christians, which starts with the life of Christ, as is prophet Muhammad for Islam. Therefore, the Christians generally follow the Bible and the life of Jesus and his teachings written in the New Testament, and Muslims follow the teachings of their prophet, Muhammad.

Religion can therefore be described as a way of connecting to the divine through the experiences of others who point out a certain way of living in order to get closer to the divine, or God. Hence there is talk of heaven and hell. If you follow and obey these rules, you get to go to heaven. If not, you rot and burn in hell. I find most religions tend to instil fear of God so people may live by their teachings.

I also find that religion can cause separateness. Throughout the ages, wars mostly stemmed from religion. Wars between Hindus and Muslims, Christians and Jews, each trying to prove their religion as the true religion. Many murders are committed in the name of religious practices.

Religion is community oriented, based on rules, and emphasizes knowledge which focuses on obedience being the way to salvation, as well as obeying the external divinity with the duality between good and evil. In the future, a person will land in heaven or hell. It encourages self-sacrifice or being dutiful and has pity on others. It is also directed by authority and based on theology.

Spirituality is based on personal beliefs and opinions. I say personal because others have their own opinions on spirituality, and I respect that. Perhaps you have your own opinion on this subject as well. Spirituality is a personal experience, and some of you may be able to resonate with me while some may not.

Even though spirituality may somehow be interconnected to religion—as some may ask others, "What is your spiritual belief?"— what they may actually be asking is, "What is your religious belief? Or, "What faith [religion] do you follow?"

As I mentioned before, spirituality is a very personal journey. It is not as formal as religion. It emphasizes wisdom more than knowledge. It is individual as opposed to community based. The goals of spirituality are freedom, love, compassion, and being of service. It focuses on feelings and experiencing internal divinity. It promotes unconditional love. It is based more on experience than theology.

Spiritual Being

What is a spiritual being? The question seems so simple, yet the answer is not as simple. Being an analytical person, the answers to any questions are never simple because I tend to overthink and overanalyse everything to death. I won't bore you with my overanalysis. I will keep it simple, though that is just as tough because I will feel that I am not giving you the full picture.

However, we know we are human beings and have learnt over our lifetimes that each of us has a soul. Our souls represent our core essences. It is also considered to be one's spirit. When our physical bodies expire, our souls live on as what we call the spirit.

There is some belief that the soul leaves the body when we die, and that's when we enter the spiritual realm as a spirit, thus the saying, "We are spiritual beings having a human experience." It is also believed that one's soul or spirit comes back to this earth in another physical body and experiences another life in a human body. It is said that we have multiple lifetimes.

Some believe that our souls can come back not only in human form but also in animal form. Although I have experienced a sense with some animals when I see them that they may have had a human experience, I am still stumped and unable to comprehend this sense that I feel. But then again, I have experienced many senses and feelings about things that cannot be logically explained.

Many people find it difficult to grasp this notion of a person having multiple lifetimes. It's difficult after all to wrap their heads around a phenomenon that cannot be explained scientifically.

Another way to look at it is as person whose lifestyle resonates with spiritual principles. They exhibit such characteristics as respect for individual beliefs, compassion, unconditional love for fellow humans, and desire to be of service to others. Such individuals are willing to help lift others up when they are down and to help people grow and become better people. I consider these individuals to be spiritual beings.

I could not find much information on what others may have expressed about what they think or know about spiritual beings to make comparisons with my opinion. This will have to suffice for now as I do not wish to impart any information I do not have or do not know. Nor do I want to make something up.

Chapter 2

Personality Types

What Are Personality Types?

The topic of personality type would be lengthy if I were to go deep into it. People are complicated, and it is impossible to understand totally a person in their entirety. No two people will have identical personalities. However, people do have some common traits due to some factors that may influence a person's personality type. Some of these are inborn.

I am going to try to keep it simple and yet give you some understanding of various personality types so you can follow what I am talking about as you walk through my spiritual journey.

There is a lot of talk about personality types. People even may have made a casual comment about a personality type whether we do or do not really understand the deep meaning of such comments. You may, for example, have heard people comment on a person's personality, saying the individual is a type A personality.

Before I understood much about personality types, whenever I heard a comment made about a person, it was about being a type A personality. When I hear this comment the traits that I noticed those of such a type—without really researching details of such types—are often structured or inflexible. They tend to like to follow a very strict schedule, are very organized, and do not like to be spontaneous. They like to plan and follow the plan they laid out for themselves. They tend to be competitive, self-critical, and goal-oriented.

Type B personalities are generally known to be relaxed, patient, and easy-going. Since they are of an easy-going nature and do not cause a stir, you are less likely to hear people make comments such as, "Oh, you must be a type B personality." When this comment may be made is when this subject is the topic of conversation, and people are analysing each other's personalities.

There is also a type C personality type which you rarely or possibly never heard of. The little that I know of this type is that they are generally overcompensating, or they can be considered people pleasers.

There is also the introvert, extrovert, and ambivert. I am sure you have heard of extrovert and introvert types, while some of you may not have heard of an ambivert. Extroverts are generally categorized as people who are friendly and outgoing, and introverts are shy and aloof. Extroverts thrive in crowds; they are energized by the energies of people around them. Introverts feel drained by the crowds. The reality is that the introverts are not shy or aloof; they can be warm and friendly. But spending too much time amongst people for too long or being in a crowded environment drains their energy.

Now ambiverts are a combination of both extrovert and introvert. This means they are comfortable in a crowded setting but only for a limited time. Then they want their alone time. Introverts generally prefer more alone time than the ambivert. The same goes for an extrovert, only the opposite of the introvert.

In my opinion, when it comes to a person's personality type, no one can really define it accurately, not even an expert psychologist. I think we can at most come to a general conclusion about personality trait based on what we observe about a person's behaviour pattern.

It is also difficult to know anyone by their behaviour alone. At times people hide their true selves and may project certain personas in one setting and a different one in others. It has been my observation of many with a social media presence that they tend to have two projections of themselves, one in real life and their social media life. In my observations, some people crave attention so desperately that they feel the need to fill their social media with every moment of their lives, no matter how insignificant the moment, and with beautiful quotes that they do not live by or believe in.

Therefore, psychology experts cannot really give accurate personality descriptions, although a commonality and a general categorization can be made. I find these interesting and undeniable and will touch on these in personality types.

Myers-Briggs Personality Types

Some of you may have heard of Myers-Briggs personality types. Katherine Briggs, impressed by Carl Jung's theory of personality types, felt the need to simplify the assessment of the personality types by grouping them according to ways that people have a tendency to think and act in important ways that identify their differences. Mother-daughter team, Katherine Briggs and Isabel Briggs Myers categorizes the personality types into four main opposing categories. These four main categories follow.

Introvert vs Extrovert

Introverts are people who tend to think, reflect, and contemplate. They tend to feel drained in crowded settings and prefer to have more alone time to recharge and regain their energies. Extroverts prefer to be in a crowded environment as they feel energized being amongst people.

Intuitive vs Sensitive

Intuitives analyse the overall pattern, its meaning, and connections. Sensors are more attuned to their environments and surroundings by relying on what they feel, see, or hear.

Thinking vs Feeling

The difference between the thinkers and feelers is the way they make their decisions. The thinkers rely on their logic; they seek logical solutions. Feelers make their decisions based on their feelings and emotions, values, and needs of others.

Perceiving vs Judging

Perceivers are more like type B personality types. They are more relaxed and flexible, and are reluctant to commit. Judgers are like the type A personality type, who prefers structure and likes things to be clearly regulated. They seldom like change and spontaneity.

The idea of categorizing people into a personality type category is to help people understand their strengths and weaknesses and how they can appreciate diversity in others.

According to Myers-Briggs' personality type theory, you are either an introvert or extrovert, sensor or perceiver, thinker or feeler. Once you understand which category resonates with or best describes you, a four-letter code is assigned to indicate your personality type, such as E for an extrovert, N for intuitive, T for thinking, and P for perceiving. So the category you fall under is ENTP ... so on and so forth.

Myers and Briggs defined sixteen personality types from the four categories mentioned previously. Following is a brief description for your quick reference.

1. ENTP—The Visionary
   They are always in search of solutions to challenging problems and are inspired innovators.

2. ENTJ—The Commander
   They are leaders and motivators and like to bring about change.

3. ENFJ—The Teacher
   They are idealists and love to serve humanity.

4. ENFP—The Champion
   They are people-oriented and motivated by their potentials and possibilities.

5. ESTJ—The Supervisor
   They like to take charge and get things done.

6. ESFJ—The Provider
   They are conscientious helpers and dedicate themselves to others.

7. ESTP—The Dynamo
   They are active, like to push their boundaries, and are thrill seekers.

8. ESFP—The Entertainer
   These types are fun loving, charming, and love to entertain.

9. ISTJ—The Inspector
   They like being organized and will effectively eliminate chaos to create organization.

10. ISFJ—The Protector
    They are responsible caretakers and very loyal to institution and tradition.

11. ISTP—The Craftsperson
    They are observant and problem-solvers; their strengths are in troubleshooting.

12. ISFP—The Composer
    They are gentle, caring, and prefer to keep a low profile.

13. INTJ—The Mastermind
    They are analytical and eager to improve processes and systems and to problem solve.

14. INTP—The Architect
    Logical analysis fascinates them. They are innovators and philosophical.

15. INFP—The Healer
    They are idealistic and imaginative, guided by their
    own values and beliefs.

16. INFJ—The Counsellor
    They have a strong sense of integrity and are creative
    nurturers.

Understanding Personality Types

Most of my life I have been a very analytical person. I spend most
of my time in my head. Psychology has been a subject of interest
for me as I have the desire to understand people so I know how to
relate to them and be able to interact and communicate effectively.

To understand people better, it is important for me to put myself into
their shoes. Being an empath—something I will talk about further
into this journey—it was not difficult for me to do so.

Due to my interest in human psychology, I was interested to learn
about personality types. But I did not put too much time in to
understanding the different personality types in my younger years as
I was too busy surviving and overcoming life challenges I was faced
with at the time. Interestingly, in the quest to learn about myself
and find my true self, I was able to observe the different personality
types, and I made mental notes of my observations. Because of my
keen observations of myself and my actions as well as those of other
people. As I mentioned earlier, I noticed people commenting about
a person being a type A personality type and so on, and this led to
my curiosity about this personality type.

I was still too deep into my own dark and challenging world at the
time (something I share in my book *Take Charge*). It did not allow

17

me the luxury of time to dive deeper into understanding the broader aspect of the different personality types. But because I always made mental notes of what I learnt along the way, I can always pull up the needed information in my mental library.

Since I started to research more and more on personality types, I took the Myers-Briggs personality types test. My most recent test result puts me in the category of the INFJ type, which seems to fit me perfectly. Yes, it does seem to describe me very well the way I am today. However, before I did all this soul searching and growing and becoming who I am today, I was different two decades ago. It occurred to me, though, that if I was somewhat different, then I should fit into a different category. Sure enough, I did in fact fit into a different category. I know this for certain because I took the Myers-Briggs personality test, when I attended a workshop at YWCA when I was considering a career change. I happened to find my test results recently and saw that my test results stated that I was an ENTP.

It made sense to me because I do recall I was far more extroverted at that time than I am now. Logic was definitely prominent, and if you have read my previous book, you know how I have described the time when logic ruled my life. I was the visionary always in search of a solution to challenging problems, and I did in dealing with my challenges.

Going through life experiences and making a conscious decision to grow and change really put me into a unique category. However, at this time of my life, I strongly resonate with being in the INFJ empath category as it fits with who I am today.

I have always been on the quest to understand personality types so I can have a better understanding of how I can communicate with people in order to have a better and harmonious relationship with mutual respect and acceptance of who we are as individuals.

My Personality Type

I have taken this Myers-Briggs personality test more than once and gotten different test results. These tests and their results were taken twenty years apart. The first result was ENTP—The Visionary. An ENTP is always in search of solutions to challenging problems. They are also inspired innovators. Present day, twenty years later, my result is INFJ—The Counsellor. An INFJ has a strong sense of integrity and is a creative nurturer. As I mentioned earlier, I was not surprised at the difference as I had changed in those intervening years.

When I retook the test and was categorized as an INFJ, I proceeded to do as much research as I could. While the traits described did indeed describe me accurately, there was more to me and my personality trait. Then I stumbled upon information about being an INFJ empath. That resonated with me even more.

Since I found out I fell into an INFJ category type, I have been on a quest to learn more about this type. Since I started to learn more about INFJs, I unintentionally came across an online group dedicated to the INFJs or another group for intuitives.

From my research, I found that both ENTP and INFJ groups are the most uncommon of all sixteen groups. Amongst the general population, about 3 per cent are categorized as ENTP; 4 per cent are men and 2 percent women. There are about 2 per cent of the general population who are INFJs, but only .05 per cent are INFJ empaths. That puts me in a rare category. I am not surprised as I always felt like the odd one out. I always felt I did not have much in common with people around me. I am what some would call not the norm. How I think and interact with people are unique. At times I felt like an outsider or even alien. In fact, I was even called an alien. I have also been told I am crazy and that my highly intuitive gifts (or even empathic gifts) are witchy stuff. If you read my previous book, you will understand how much I have worked on myself to be where I am today as a person.

Having gone through my life experiences, I have learned to accept everything about myself and who I am. All of the efforts I put in being who I am today helped me to accept everything about myself, so there is not much anyone can say to me to put me down. When I am told I am crazy, I respond with, "Tell me something I don't know."

I encourage you to go within. Understand who you are, and accept everything about yourself. Be comfortable with who you are with all the perks and quirks that come with being you. If you do, then no one can crush you because you are fine being who you are. You are enough.

Fitting into More Than One Category

As mentioned previously, according to the tests I have taken, I fall under the two least populated categories— ENTP and INFJ, or INFJ empath. Here I discuss in more detail the two categories to give you more clarity about these two types. Those of you who know me now or have known me for years should be able to see these traits in me and know how accurately I fall under these categories.

What is ENTP all about? E (extroverted), N (intuition), T (thinking), P (perceiving). ENTPs are extroverted, intuitive, thinking, open-minded, and unconventional. They like to understand and are very analytical, so they always want to analyse and influence other people. They are eccentric, cheerful, and fun. They often poke fun at themselves. ENTPs are nonjudgemental and the live-and-let-live type.

They prefer to focus on concepts and ideas and are creative and flexible. Therefore they dislike rigidity and like to be spontaneous. I have really been spontaneous all my life. I am creative and tend to analyse everything to death. Some of you have even commented that I analyse things to a minute atom or even ask me why I need to analyse everything.

ENTPs are visionaries and have a passion for new ideas and innovation. ENTPs are also great at problem-solving. They thrive on and are inspired to problem solve issues others may find challenging, but ENTPs are energized by challenges. They have confidence in themselves and in their abilities to adapt to new situations. I find this to be very true because I am always in my head, finding ways to overcome challenges and solutions to my problems or of those around me. People usually come to me when they are seeking answers to their problems.

Visionaries like to come up with better and faster ways to do things, hence they do not like the restrictive established way of doing things. This is so true of me, especially at work, I like to be efficient and am always thinking of ways I can work better and faster. This is one of my strengths in my profession and one for which I am well known. So much so I even earned a few nicknames for my efficiency, like Speedy Gonzales, fast train, blur, 3 in 1, machine, and alien.

ENTPs are quick-witted and have incisive humour. They are always curious about the world and want to know how things work. They do not like to follow any set of rules that could be limiting. I agree. I prefer to do things my way because I know how I operate and how I can do things faster and better based on my nature. And I know what works best for me to arrive at the result we want, so I do have a tendency to work differently.

ENTPs are generally entrepreneurial, creative, friendly, resourceful, headstrong, independent, and have the highest ability to cope with stress. This is something I am sure you will agree with if you know me or you can understand how this is true about me after you read my book *Take Charge*.

Now more about INFJ. INFJ I (introverted), N (intuitive), F (feeling), J (judging). This type is generally caring, creative, highly sensitive, and reserved. They have the ability to read others and can see behind the masks people unconsciously put on. They have many layers that they reveal slowly, if ever.

Their main function is the introverted intuition (IN). Because of this, they may sometimes be considered to have psychic ability, though it may not be truly the case. They are highly perceptive of others and can see the bigger picture. But they can easily miss the minute detail, such as remembering someone's birthday. This type tends to absorb and sense others' feelings and emotions.

They not only sense people's emotional and mental states, they tend to feel all of these literally in their bodies which can be overwhelming. They can use this ability to heal others by jumping deep into their suffering. Now this is something you know is part of my personality if you happen to be in my social or professional circles.

Having clarity about these two personality types, and me knowing who I am, I can safely say that I do fit into more than one category type.

What More to the Personality Type?

The INFJ, being the highly intuitive and highly sensitive type, tends to be very empathic. They can sense and feel people's emotions and mental states. But while INFJs are empathic, not all INFJs are empaths.

The empaths, just like the INFJ, can sense and feel the mental and emotional states of others in their bodies, they also can sense and feel the physical states of others. The physical pain and symptoms of others are also felt in their own bodies, which again can be very overwhelming for an empath. Empaths are bombarded by multitudes of emotional pain and physical pain of other people whether they are in close physical proximity or at a distance.

I feel the mental, emotional, and physical pains of people I know, even when they are overseas. I am at times able to feel when something happens to my loved ones, near or far, as it is happening. Sometimes I even feel their thoughts. At times I can feel when someone is lying to me or about to lie to me.

Because it is rare, some would say being an INFJ empath is a gift. Some may even say that it is a spiritual gift. It is a gift because it helps me to feel and sense what others around me are feeling, so it helps me to be better able to understand them and be more sympathetic. Being a holistic healer, I am able to know and feel what ails a person and am able to help in the healing process.

However, it is not always fun. At times it feels more of a curse, as some would put it, or a double-edged sword. Because I literally feel others' emotional, mental, and physical pain, can be very draining and difficult. In reality, it can be *extremely* difficult.

Before I was aware of this gift, I didn't know what was happening. I did not understand why I was feeling what I was feeling, even though I had analysed my circumstances and knew I really had no valid reasons for all these emotional and physical pains that would come on suddenly.

There were times I felt debilitated by all of these, especially since I was going through my own physical health issues, and at times I felt like it was driving me to the edge. I feel fortunate that I had within me a very strong faith that kept me going. I also have inner guidance, or what I would say my guardian angels, that helped me through the trying times.

Now that you have some understanding of my personality type and how it fits me, this may trigger you to want to understand your personality type. You may even consider taking the Myers-Briggs test to see if the result resonates with you. I encourage you to do so. When you understand your type or yourself, it may encourage and help you to understand people of other types. When you start to research types of personalities, you may come to understand people better who are in your circle. It will also help you to understand how to relate to people you may encounter. I believe when you have a better understanding of yourself and others, it will help bring about harmony and peace in your world.

Chapter 3

Empaths

What Does It Mean to Be an Empath?

Being an empath is different than being empathetic. An empath is someone who has the gift of absorbing the energies of their surroundings, including the energies of people, plants, and animals.

Empaths are known to be highly sensitive individuals. They can sense and feel what people are thinking or feeling. Empaths are known to experience a great deal of empathy to the point of taking the pain of others as their own. I can relate to this. I can often feel what a person is going through. I can feel their emotions, be it sadness, anger, or joy.

I also feel the physical symptoms of people I know, including pain, nausea, or fever. They do not need to be near me; I can feel or sense someone's pain and emotions from a distance, even overseas. The closer the relationship or the bond I have with them—for example, family members or close friends—the stronger or more frequently I can feel what is happening with them. I can pick up the emotions or pains of strangers only if they are in close proximity. Sometimes it is difficult to know whose energies I am picking up on while I am feeling them. However, there are times I can feel whose energy I am experiencing. I noticed this is possible when I have a closer bond with the individual. Then I know what the person is feeling emotionally or physically.

At times I can feel people's thoughts whether they choose to express them verbally or not. And when I am asked something, I can feel if the questions are in fact not coming from the person asking but from a third party who is not comfortable asking me directly. This is why some empaths are considered to be like human lie detectors. I often can sense when someone feeds me lies or is about to lie to me. When I feel someone is about to feed me lies, I make strong eye contact with the person. Somehow that seems to deter someone from doing so. However, that doesn't mean I can accurately detect every lie fed to me. Some people are so good and convincing that their lies miss my radar. I think when lies miss my radar it is because I am a very trusting person and like to give people the benefit of the doubt. I choose not to be sceptical of people all the time. I prefer to look for the good in people rather than be suspicious of people's motives.

Being an empath and able to sense people's emotions and pains can be overwhelming and at times difficult to bear, especially if I am absorbing energies of multiple people. It may cause me to wake up several times in the night. Having a knowing of something can also be bothersome because it can make me anxious wondering why I know what I know and if it is, in fact, a reality or my imagination. Even though I may have confirmation of my senses, I still at times hope it is my imagination, especially if it is something that is not positive.

At times I feel a heavy responsibility being an empath because I feel the need to help and make things better for people, mostly with difficult cases; I do not give up on them. But most times it is a pleasure to help. It feels good to know that I am able to make a difference in people's lives.

Empaths are generally good listeners. People are somehow drawn to empaths and find it comfortable to dump their worries on them, even when they may be meeting for the first time.

For years I struggled because I was unaware of why I was feeling the way I did. Why did I know what happened between people before I walked into the room? Why did I feel people's emotions and pains? For a long time, I did not know how to manage or deal with all the things that were coming towards me.

It took me years to understand that I can somehow manage and live without being too affected or overwhelmed by the energies I am picking up. I have learnt to differentiate between my energies and those of the others. Being somewhat able to know if the pains and emotions I am feeling are mine or not has made things comfortable and manageable.

Empath vs Empathy

To have empathy is similar to having sympathy. Everyone has the capability to empathize or sympathize except for the psychopaths.

Empathy is the ability to understand circumstances or feelings others are going through, feeling in tune with people's emotions. An empathic person can be moved by a heart-tugging situation that gives rise to a feeling of compassion and kindness, like when a person's heart goes out to another about what another is going through due to circumstances.

Empaths not only feel empathy for others, but they feel it more to the next level. They are able to feel what others feel or are feeling in their own bodies. This can be deemed as extraordinary empathy.

An empath absorbs the energy of people which causes them to feel what the other person is feeling from joy or happy emotions to sad and unhappy or angry emotions. They can pick up physical symptoms of the other person as well, such as headache, nausea, or heart palpitations.

As stated earlier, if an empath has a strong and close relationship with someone, they can pick up the other person's energy even from long distance. I have experienced this with my own family when they were overseas or physically apart. Physical distance does not matter to an empath.

Every empath has inborn abilities to absorb energy differently. Therefore, some would define them as different types of empaths. However, I feel all empaths may experience most of the different energy absorption but may feel more in one area over another.

To help understand the strengths of one's empathic gifts, I will just call them the different types of empath. However, if you are an empath, you may have the ability to sense them all. But the list will help you to understand your strengths and how you are able to absorb the energy of your surroundings.

Types of Empaths

There are various types of empaths. I have listed them below to help you understand the differences. Some empaths may have various empathic gifts, while others may have limited traits.

Physical Receptive Empath

These are people who are able to absorb the energy of the physical conditions of others, such as the ability to feel pain and illnesses of others in their own physical bodies. Such gifts are useful for empaths who are in the healing professions as they are able to feel what the person is experiencing physically and know when they feel relief.

Emotional Receptive Empath

Emotional receptive empaths have the ability to feel emotions of other people as if their own. The joys and sorrows are felt first-hand. Most empaths have the tendency to feel both. It is just a matter of which receptivity is stronger. By stronger I mean which is felt the most.

Claircognizant Empath

The claircognizant empaths have the ability to know situations or events without any rational explanation. They can know if something is impending and whether something needs to be done. They are capable of knowing if someone is being honest or not. They are like a human lie detector.

Geomantic Empath

Such empaths sense the environment. They have the ability to sense the shift in the energy vibration of the earth and so are able to sense an impending natural disaster through the energy emitted from the soil or the earth and shift in the air pattern. Such empaths are what can be termed as natural human weather forecasters.

Fauna Empath

Very in tune with the animals, such empaths have the ability to hear, sense, and feel animals. They are able to interact with them very well, and animals have a tendency to be drawn to them. However, when such empaths are upset or angry, they may scare the animals. The animals may then avoid them as animals can sense their disturbing energies.

Medium Empath
People who have the ability to sense, see, feel, or hear spirits are known as medium empaths. They are also able to feel the emotions of the spirits that are around them.

Flora Empath
Flora empaths have the ability to sense and feel the plants and receive signals from the plants.

Psychometric Empath
Psychometric empaths read energies of inanimate objects such as jewellery, furniture, and photographs. They either feel the impression or have the ability to see the vision of the impression left behind from the object.

Telepathic Empath
Telepathic empaths can read unexpressed thoughts of others fairly accurately.

Precognitive Empath
These empaths can sense an event or situation before it occurs. These will occur in the forms of dreams or intense physical or emotional sensations.

Heyoka Empath
Heyoka empaths can block emotions and project mirror emotions of others onto themselves, which is thought-provoking. They heal others through humour, hence "heyoka" is a Native American term for a sacred clown. They also have the ability to heal others in ways that people are receptive to.

Multipotentialite Empath
Multipotentialite empaths are hardwired into learning. They have the ability to absorb everything around them. They do not have

one true vocation. They thrive on learning and acquiring new skills and are able to master them all. Thus, it helps them to be able to help others on multiple levels due to their insatiable desires to learn and constantly absorb new skills. They have a wealth of knowledge that gives them the ability to help people from all walks of life in all areas of their lives.

What Type of Empath Am I?

Like myself, some empaths will most likely resonate with more than one type because their abilities will overlap. Different types of empaths will have strengths in different areas. Some may feel the emotions of others more strongly than in other areas. Some may be more drawn or connected to animals and plants. These fauna empaths have the capacity to understand the mental and emotional states of animals. I feel that I don't have this type developed, although I do feel that animals tend to feel drawn to me. But I do not think I can read them as well as some others can.

I can read people better than I can animals. I believe I have some telepathic abilities, mainly with those I am close to. I feel plants tend to connect with me somehow; I feel emotional when a plant or tree gets chopped. I also notice that my plants are affected by situations occurring in my life. They thrive beautifully when positive events are happening in my life, and they get sick when I am going through rough times. I really do not know how to explain this. Being an empath, I should be feeling what the plant is feeling. I do somewhat, but in my observations, my plants are more affected by what is happening around me.

I resonate mostly with being a multipotentialite empath, physical perceptive, emotional perceptive, claircognizant, and medium empath. And vaguely on the rest, except for geomantic. I do not sense the changes of earth energies. This is one area I do not feel anything as long as I can remember. I am not able to forecast changes in weather or disturbances within the earth or environment.

Being a multipotentialite empath can be somewhat challenging because I am so hardwired to learn, constantly needing to absorb new information, have multiple interests, and am not satisfied with limited information. I want to excel in everything I get my hands into, and boy, do I want to get my hands into many things! Learning new things excites me, and I feel I want to pursue whatever comes my way, so I do not have just one calling in life.

That's probably why I am in various professions and multiple hobbies: floral designer, holistic practitioner, makeup artist, hairstylist, accounting, arts and crafts, author. I feel there is always something new to learn. I like to challenge myself most times just to know if I have the ability or can learn and absorb something new. I do not have issues with most things.

My biggest weakness is anything to do with technology. Perhaps I do not have a strong interest in it, so I have a tendency to forget what I learnt. My main interest is in people. I like to understand and learn anything I can about them, for example the how and why they think and act the ways they do.

Top on my list are emotional and physical perception. Being a holistic practitioner, this is helpful as it gives me the upper hand to understand what a person is going through and what they are feeling so I can better help the individual when doing a healing session.

Chapter 4

My Personality Type

What Type Am I?

Since I have given you some basic understanding of the various personality types, I can now delve deeper into what personality type I am, which may help in understanding my life's journey or my spiritual journey. I am sure you know that we are all going through our own journeys according to what we believe in or what resonates with us.

You may already know the path you are on. Or maybe you are just trying to understand what path you are on or want to be on. If you are like me, always doing self-analysis, then you probably already know about your own journeys. I believe it is my interest to do self-analysis so I can better understand myself. This allows me to better understand others, so I know how I can effectively connect and communicate with people I come into contact with, and it led me to understand and find out more about my personality type.

As mentioned earlier, I did the Myers-Briggs personality tests twice, twenty years apart, which showed two different results, ENTP and INFJ. When we read about the two personality types, I can say they both fit who I am today, with some changes of course. I would say I am currently an ambivert, which is having the characteristics of both extroverts and introverts. But I feel more of an introvert as I prefer alone time and feel drained after spending time with people. I think that is probably the reason my current tests put me in the INFJ category.

Although most INFJs are empathic, it does not mean they are all empaths. I know I am an empath because of my life experiences, as I have mentioned earlier. Therefore, I can be categorized as an INFJ empath putting me in the .05 per cent of the world population.

Being a person in a rare category and spending years overcoming life challenges has helped me to be a confident and strong person. Because of this, I probably carry myself in a certain way. Unbeknownst to me, some people tend to find my demeanour intimidating when they first meet me.

I am also told that after the initial misunderstanding of me as intimidating, people often find me to be like a marshmallow. Yet there are also people who find me warm, caring, and approachable. It feels comfortable for them to spill their beans and share their most personal issues on our first meeting, as if they have known me their entire lifetimes. This happens to be true for empaths. People feel drawn to them and start to share. Most empaths are in the healing professions because we are what you call a natural in healing work.

Carl Jung or Myers and Briggs may have come up with the theory of personality types based on what I assume is the personality type a person is born with. By understanding our personality types, we will have clarity on our strengths and weaknesses to build our characters. To become the person, we would like to be. To be true to ourselves and to be authentic and happy.

If I were to describe myself, or what personality type I am, I can easily say I fall into a complex category. I would humorously say I am one of a kind, unique, or not the norm. I have accepted that I am not the norm and am good with that. The reason is that I have consciously decided to be the person I want to be by understanding the personality type I was born with.

Since I have accepted who I am as I am, I love the person I am. I know how to make myself happy. When we love ourselves and are happy, we can spread love and happiness unto others.

How Am I Different?

How am I different from the rest of the personality types? As previously mentioned, I received different results on the personality tests I took twenty years apart. And when I examine myself today, I still have the traits of both personality types, so I guess I can say the two types blended. Plus, my gifts as an empath have grown stronger over the years. I have met some people who have taken the Myers-Briggs personality tests and found they are INFJ, and few others I have met fall into a different category, but I have not yet met anyone who may have taken a test at different times and get different results.

If I were to go back in time to when I started to be curious about having a better understanding of myself and examine it now, I think that is probably the time I may have started my spiritual awakening which led me to my spiritual journey. But if I were to really dive deep into my past to my childhood years, I believe I have always been spiritual but not really aware of it. Or should I say as aware about going on a spiritual path or journey as I am today?

I have to admit that as a child, I did like the spiritual way of life because I was always interested in being of service to others and helping the less fortunate. That was why I was so interested in the way nuns lived. They dedicated their lives to service of God and his people. I was so drawn to the way they lived to spend their time helping all those in need that I considered joining the convent. But that did not happen as my parents arranged my marriage.

My book *Take Charge* covers the earlier years of my life and how I faced and overcame life challenges. It also helps you to understand me and my life, and how it shaped me differently from the rest of the personality types. I spent a fair number of years understanding who I am, discovering my authentic self, and understanding my life's purpose. The feedback I received from *Take Charge* was that it was soul searching as well as inspiring, motivating, and uplifting.

I would say I may have been on my spiritual journey all my life only to become more aware of it in the last two decades. Since I made a conscious decision to grow and be more aligned with spirituality, I feel that makes me different from the rest of the personality types. However, I am sure there are also many of you who may have done the same for yourself, and that would make you unique in your own way.

Then there are also some of you looking for some answers and guidance in how to find yourself. I congratulate you for taking the steps towards your journey of being you and who you want to be, and what path you want to take in this lifetime. I will be honoured to be there for you should you like any assistance in finding your way and want me to assist you. It will be my pleasure to share whatever knowledge I have gained in my journey to help you with yours.

The Path I Walk

What is it really like to be in my shoes? In order for me to share with you what it is really like to be in my shoes, I will dig deeper into my life to tell you what it is like.

When you first meet me, there is no way you can imagine the life I have had, the struggles, the challenges, and the fears I faced. When someone meets me, what they see is how I am now, what they perceive me to be, and how I approach life or handle life's situations. I am told I am a person with a positive outlook and with a cheerful and calm demeanour.

It is not easy for anyone to guess that I have gone through enormous struggles in life because I did not allow any challenges to affect me negatively. You may have heard that life's events can either make you a bitter person or a better person. I chose to be better.

So, what is it really like to walk my path as an INFJ empath? It certainly is not a bed of roses; there are advantages and disadvantages. As explained previously, being a highly sensitive person and empath, I can sense and feel people's physical and emotional pain.

Just try and imagine what it must be like to be in pain constantly and not know why. The worst part is before I was aware of this gift, I was in constant search for the reasons I felt what I was feeling, the pain I was experiencing. Doctor to doctor, test after test, and there was no medical reason for my pain.

I did have a health condition called endometriosis (plus other health issues) that caused excruciating chronic pain. It was not easily diagnosed in my earlier years. The only possible way to diagnose it was through laparoscopic surgery at the time. I struggled with constant undiagnosed pain of my own plus picking up on not just one other person's physical and emotional pains, but the pains of multiple people at the same time. Something that can be considered a double whammy.

Being an ENTP puts me into a thinker category; that is, I am logical, analytical, and like to analyse things to the minute detail. You can safely imagine how I probably drove myself insane by always being in my head. My friends who know this about me used to say to me, "You are your own worst enemy by trying to analyse everything to death."

For a long while, it was difficult being in this body that was experiencing my own personal emotional and physical pain as well as those that did not belong to me. In my quest to find myself and reclaim my life, I became more aware of myself, what I resonated with, and what and how it affected me.

I came to understand the gift I was born with. Being an empath is considered a spiritual gift. It took me years to become aware of who I am or what my path is in this life. In a way I would say I have been on my spiritual journey all along. I just was not quite aware of it because I was too busy prioritizing, sorting out my life's path.

Currently, I am happy to say that because I have a clear understanding of who I am and how I am in different circumstances and accepting everything about myself, I would say I am comfortable and happy walking this path.

Advantages or Blessings

It is a fact that there are two sides to everything—two polarities, front and back, positive and negative, strengths and weaknesses, advantages and disadvantages. Like everything else, there are advantages and disadvantages to every personality type.

On a positive note, the advantages of being an INFJ empath is a blessing or a gift. Some advantages are being strong-willed, decisive, and having a conviction to pursue goals with great efficiency.

Due to my determination, I follow through with everything I set my mind to, and have the patience to inspire and guide others with deep and insightful understanding. Because of my empathic gift and being an INFJ, also known as a counsellor, I have the natural ability to help with emotional challenges a person is going through.

We are also known to be intellectual and like to know how to deal with challenges. We are creative and problem-solve. I find that in my employment, I am often sought out to find ways to tackle challenging tasks and come up with creative methods to produce some designs. I can always come up with ideas on how to be efficiently creative, which is the way I like to work.

Having creative and artistic gifts, I enjoy dabbling in arts and crafts. I find it very comforting to be lost in my creations, be it crocheting, sewing, crafting, painting, or designing. For me, during the most painful and challenging times of my life, this creative gift has been a lifesaver.

I found inspiration to be exceptionally creative, and I often got lost in my creation which provided relief from what I was going through. Therefore, I would consider this a blessing because in all honesty, I really do not know how I would have survived all that I lived through.

Having the ability to sense and feel in my body what others are feeling, I am able to know what another person is going through. And having compassion, it makes it possible for me to comfort and heal anyone who seeks out my help. I feel blessed to know that I can touch lives around me in a positive way.

It is very rewarding for me when I have confirmation and can actually witness the change, I have brought into someone's life and know the person feels better and happier. Along the way, through the healing work that I do, I have met so many wonderful people and have established great friendships that feel like family to me.

I feel very fortunate to be an empath. I am happy with who I am.

Disadvantages

We all know that there are disadvantages to everything. Yes, as much as I do feel lucky and blessed to be who I am, there is a definite disadvantage. You are probably wondering how or why, especially since I just mentioned that I feel fortunate and happy to be me.

The disadvantage is what I call the dark side of being an INFJ empath, the struggles we go through being who we are. You already understand that I feel emotions and pains of others along with my own. Before I was aware of the fact that I was absorbing all the energies around me, and as I mentioned previously, I experienced all kinds of physical ailments on a regular basis and would end up going to doctors and get numerous tests only to find nothing. This was not exactly a fun process since it seemed that I was only going to doctors for attention. It was frustrating not to be able to find the cause of my issues. Then there was also the issue of my own health condition, undiagnosed endometriosis. So, all these health problems—mine as well as those that did not belong to me—became overwhelming and debilitating. But due to my determined nature (a blessing), I did my best to function.

I felt the emotional pain of a mother at my workplace whose daughter was diagnosed with cancer. I cried every day when I got home. The grief I felt was so great that I had to resign from the job to distance myself. At the time, I did not know how to manage the gift I had or how to not take on the pain and emotions that did not belong to me.

There were times when I went to work only to feel something. Sometimes I felt the heaviness and discomfort in the energy of a room I entered where arguments had just taken place. I feel the discomfort of knowing and sensing people around me who feel envious, angry, or upset.

When it is compounded by the emotions of multiple people, it is extremely difficult because I exert a lot of energy trying to just ignore what I am experiencing. Sometimes I even pretend I don't feel the emotions. Dealing with others' emotions can leave me exhausted at the end of the day.

Being a determined person, I do not give up on anything I do. Along with being decisive, if I decide to do any project with a deadline, I will not give up on until I meet that deadline even if it means not taking any breaks, meals, or sleep. I am sure you will agree this is not good for me, so we can certainly agree that this is a definite disadvantage.

Aside from being an INFJ empath, I do fit into multipotentialite empath in the empath category. This means that I tend to have multiple interests and multiple paths and a constant need and desire to learn anything and everything that piques my interests, or even anything I feel I should learn. You can imagine my brain never stops. It's always on the go. I have even been told, "Your brain never stops," or, "Give your brain a rest."

It can be tough at times that my brain and my body are always on the go. I feel I must not waste any precious moments I have, and this can lead me to burning out. And yet at times I do not let it stop me from carrying on. Fortunately, I am learning to respect my body, trying to take care of myself more, and getting the necessary rest when needed.

I am being kinder to myself now. I am more attuned to my body. The senses that I feel are mine or not mine, and I am trying to not let things that do not belong to me affect me mentally, physically, and emotionally. This has helped me to be healthier, happier, and more empowered.

I highly recommend that you learn to be more in tune with yourself— who you are and what is good for you physically, emotionally, and mentally. And take care of you so you are healthier, happier, and more at peace.

Chapter 5

Spiritual Gifts

What Is a Spiritual Gift?

When I started to write this book and wrote out this chapter title, my version of spiritual gifts or the understanding of spiritual gifts based on my perspective of the concept of spiritual gifts from my own experiences. As I started to write about this topic, I felt the need to research the meaning of spiritual gifts as is available on the internet. Most of it was information being written with reference to the Bible or in connection to church ministries.

Although I was raised Catholic and was interested in joining a convent, I feel I do not want to talk about spiritual gifts with references to any biblical quotes as I do not wish to quote something that I feel I am not personally familiar with in the Bible itself. I prefer to share information on this topic based on my experience and knowledge.

When I started to write this book, I did do some research to help me express my thoughts on my experiences as I went along each chapter. With this chapter I just felt I could find information that spoke to me in ways that could help me express it as easily as other research, I have done.

I will do my best to explain to you what I think spiritual gifts are based on my experience. Just remember this is simply my opinions and thoughts of what spiritual gifts mean to me in my life. It is possible that some of you may have a similar opinion on this or perhaps a slightly different version of it. However, I think it is commonly known that being an empath, or a medium (a person who can connect to the spirits who have moved on from this physical life), is considered a spiritual gift. As are the abilities to have prophetic dreams; to heal; counsel; see visions of future events; to have a sense (clairsentient) or knowing of something and not know why you know (claircognizant); and to hear sounds, conversations, or messages from other realms (clairaudient).

There has been mention of other gifts, such as to counsel or teach, speak in different tongues, interpret tongues, wisdom, and knowledge. I feel God has gifted us these abilities to help and serve humankind. The Holy Spirit assists us to use our gifts for the good of humankind, to be loving and caring towards each other.

Different people possess different gifts depending on the paths they are supposed to be on and how they are to help fellow beings. Some may have very specific paths, so they will have specific gifts. Others may have multiple paths and will possess multiple gifts to be able to serve others accordingly.

Do I Have Spiritual Gifts?

Now that you have some understanding of the different spiritual gifts people possess, it will be easier for you to have a better understanding of whether you have any spiritual gifts. Being a multipotentialite empath, I would say I have multiple gifts. I feel I had experiences of having to help people in various ways, so in order to be able to help people in different areas of life, I needed to have different gifts.

I had prophetic dreams in my childhood, but I have not had any in recent years. I have always felt, sensed, had visions, and had a sense of knowing. For me, clairsentient is more prominent than clairvoyance and claircognizant.

I have the gift of speaking multiple languages, so I can safely say I am multilingual. Although there is information online that talks about one of the spiritual gifts is the ability to speak in tongues, I am not sure if it is referred to as speaking in different languages. I am not sure if I feel I can call that one of my spiritual gifts because honestly, I don't know how it can be categorized as one.

Wisdom was also referred to as a spiritual gift. I can relate to this because I feel our guides or guardian angels do speak through us words of wisdom, thus we can consciously channel our guides during our everyday conversations. I experienced this in my younger years.

I often wondered how words of wisdom would flow out of me when I was asked for advice by my friends. And within moments, words of wisdom flowed out of me. That took me by surprise as I knew I did not have time to process any information before speaking. The knowledge I spoke also seemed to me beyond my years. But I just shrugged it off as being smart and did not know how smart I was (humorously).

I have connected with the spirits of loved ones of my friends and acquaintances.

The gift of healing is something I did not know I had in my younger years. But if I were to look back to my teenage years, I had a knowing about how the foot is the map of the body, and if we worked on certain points on our foot, we could relieve any physical discomfort in one's body. I used to practice this on one of my siblings.

I am told that I have the gift of bringing comfort and healing through my speaking, that I am a good listener, and that I give advice that helps with emotional healing. I was told that my presence seems to have a calming effect on the person or people around me. Friends and colleagues have said that when they have told me about their pains while with me, they feel their pains have been relieved soon after.

Besides being able to feel people's emotional and physical pain as if they were my own, at times I can feel their thoughts.

I have been a conscious channel but didn't realize it until about a decade ago. Later I realized I was a trance channel. We were practicing meditation, and I went into a trance momentarily and channelled messages for someone in the group I was in to practice our spiritual gifts at a spiritualist church.

When Did I Discover I Had These Gifts?

It took me years to really understand or be aware that I had these gifts. When I first realized I had the gifts, I admit I was not all willing to accept the fact that I had gifts not everyone I knew had. To answer the question "When did I discover I had these gifts?" I must backtrack into my life events to reveal the signs of having them.

When I was about 6 or 7 years old, I was ill with typhoid fever. I woke up in the middle of the night with fever as high as 40°C (104°F). I found myself sitting on what seemed to be a green cloud or an atmosphere of green energies. I sat there for quite some time before I found myself back in bed, trying to wake my elder sister as I was burning up. When I was about 8 years old, my family and I were living in Khulna, Bangladesh, when civil war broke out between the Hindus and Muslims. First the Hindus were killing Muslims. And in the middle of the night, the military took away Muslim families for protection.

My father owned a shoe shop, and someone had given him the news that one of his clients/friends had been killed. I overheard this conversation, and the same night I had a dream that this man, who was supposed to have been killed by the Hindus, was in fact alive and would visit in three months' time. That dream came true. I had other dreams that also became realities.

As for my sense of knowing—claircognizant—gift, I remember clearly when I was about 16 years old. I was in my college years, and as I was working on my school assignment, I felt my heart skip a beat. I felt a strong knowing that my brother was in an automobile accident and checked the time on my watch to see what time I felt my heart skip.

I anxiously waited for my brother to return home. I was afraid to let anyone in my family know about my feeling of a strong knowing that my brother was in an accident. After waiting anxiously for three hours, my brother finally returned home, and my sense of knowing was confirmed. He had indeed had an accident at the time my heart skipped.

When I look back throughout my life, there have been many experiences that would confirm that I had spiritual gifts since I was a child. I had prophetic dreams in my earlier years from my childhood till my mid- to late-twenties. Currently, I sense energies more than I did before. Working with energies and doing energy healings have helped me to feel and sense energies stronger than before.

Jacinta Yang

What Is It Like Having These Gifts?

I am sure many of you wonder what it would be like to have such gifts. To some of you who may not have these gifts, you may think it's so cool. Some may say, "I don't really want to know things," because you are scared to sense, feel, or know the future or to see or sense spirits. Yet there are those of you who are reading this book who most likely have or are discovering that you have a gift. You are now trying to understand yourself and to manage and deal with your gift.

Then there are some of you who have known for a while and have been living with these gifts, understanding fully that they can sometimes feel like blessings, curses, or double-edged swords due to their advantages and disadvantages.

I shall share with you my experience of what it was like and is like.

Since I used to have prophetic dreams, I would at times wake up crying from a bad dream, afraid of it coming true. At times I was afraid to have dreams. The last prophetic dream I had that came true that I did not want to come true was when I dreamt of my father passing and that I had made the funeral arrangements even though I was the youngest child.

When I go to work, there are days when I walk into the room, can feel the tense air, and know that an argument has just occurred— even though people act like nothing has happened prior to my walking in. Sadly, I can feel the uncomfortable energy in the room for hours.

To sense and feel people's feelings of envy towards me for just being me or what I am capable of doing was and remains tough. Being different or being considered different was not easy when I was not ready to accept my gifts. I was teased as being crazy or for my "witchy stuff". Once I accepted my gifts and became happy with being who I am, the teasing did not matter anymore. I would humorously respond, "Tell me something I don't know," to comments about being crazy.

Speaking of crazy, I think I do drive myself crazy being in my head a lot. Having a creative nature, my head is always spinning and thinking of all kinds of creative ideas and wanting to put them into reality. Once I figure out how I want to make something creative, with crafts or anything else, I feel the strong need to get started and get my hands into putting my vision into reality. It does not matter what time of the day it is. And if I am determined to complete the project, I won't stop until I am finished.

This is how I end up burning myself out. I do the same when I am at my job. I do not stop till I get the job done on time. I feel a strong responsibility towards anything I do. Clients have the comfort of knowing that I am reliable and will get the job done on time, even if it means I do not stop for any breaks because I am trying to beat the clock.

I sometimes feel kind and compassionate, efficient and hardworking individuals tend to be taken for granted or even taken advantage of. However, now I have worked on being empowered as well as with my gifts, I am taking better care of myself. And I do not allow anything or anyone that does not resonate with me or be good for me into my life.

I have learnt to manage my gifts and am able to separate the pains and feelings that do not belong to me most of the time. But there are still times when it's not entirely easy to do so. I can still feel overwhelmed at times, and I just allow some time to let it pass.

Being in crowded places is not comfortable because of the multitude of energies I feel and sense, so I seldom subject myself to such an environment. I do not like going into malls and avoid cramped spaces as well. I love being in nature. I prefer a calm and peaceful existence.

When Did I Accept My Gifts?

I mentioned earlier that I have experienced my gifts from a very young age but did not put much thought into, and life just carried on. But throughout my life, I have experienced my gifts. But they were just like a part of me, and I thought nothing special of them. I knew I was different, felt different, and thought differently.

I tried to ignore my gifts as if they really weren't of any importance as circumstances of life took precedence over the spiritual experiences that I encountered. However, I have had many spiritual experiences which are definitely hard to forget or ignore.

In my mid-thirties I started to experience more and more spiritual experiences and met people who were more spiritual. Books and information started to come to my attention. It was difficult for me to ignore.

I felt I was being somehow led to become more aware of my gifts. Situations and circumstances led me to delve into alternative healing to help alleviate suffering from my medical conditions. This led to my education in reiki and reflexology, a type of alternative healing. This was something that I practiced occasionally alongside my profession as a floral designer.

When I practiced reiki, my gifts of clairvoyance and mediumship opened. At first, I thought I was imagining things. Since I am a creative person, I thought I had a good imagination and shrugged it off. Over time, the experiences became too frequent for me to ignore. I reveal these experiences in detail in the next chapter.

I tried to ignore the thought that I had some sort of gift because it did not make any sense; there were no logical explanations to any of these experiences. Being a logical type, it was difficult to make sense of it, and I needed to make sense.

Interestingly, I started to encounter people in my life who could point me towards finding information on all the things happening with me. They did not really know what I was experiencing; it was just through conversations. Some books were also recommended as good reads. I took the recommendations and soon discovered information that helped me understand the reasons for my experiences.

I must admit I was still not all that eager to accept my gifts, even though I found my healing gifts were helping people in many ways. I found over time my gift of healing was helping people to heal emotionally, even though I started out with the idea of healing physical conditions.

The more I used my healing gifts through reiki, the stronger my other gifts became. I was still sceptical about all this, despite seeing the results of the work I did. My friend told me that after so much proof that I had a gift, I must learn to accept it and not doubt it.

I often get intuitive knowing of something, and when I ignore it, I later realize I should have listened to my inner voice. I gradually accepted my gift and allowed myself not to have to make sense of these spiritual gifts and experiences.

I find that when I stop questioning it too much or try to make sense of it and just accept my gifts and work with them to help others, life flows with less struggle. I can't explain it logically, but what I feel is that if I were to live my life following my spiritual journey, then things will just fall into place for me. And I feel it has. The best way to describe it is that I am swimming with the flow rather than against the current.

Chapter 6

My Spiritual Journey

Beginning

I was raised Catholic and followed the faith. In my earlier years of life, I was a devout Catholic so much so that I considered becoming a nun. Surprised? Yes, I did. I attended Catholic missionary school and spent a lot of time with the nuns in school. My observations of the nuns were that they were so loving, compassionate, and giving. And they dedicated their lives to serving humanity. They left their families to be part of a group of people of God and dedicate their lives to helping and serving others. I loved the idea of being of service to humankind and wanted to be just like them.

I wanted to be able to do what they did with their lives. I got to know everything about the nuns' lives, what they did and how they lived. So, in a way, my spiritual journey started when I was quite young, I was just not aware that this was the spiritual path. It was just a way of life I wanted for myself.

I joined the Red Crescent Society (extension of the Red Cross) in school instead of being in Girl Guides because I wanted to be able to help the poor. I was appointed treasurer of the Red Crescent Society in school and took an active role as a responsible treasurer to generate funds for our mission to help students in the villages.

I organized fundraising events in school, including plays I directed and for which I planned rehearsals. I even went fundraising door to door. It was always so exciting when I was able to raise some money for the cause our school's Red Crescent Society organized.

I feel I started my spiritual journey more on a conscience level when I started to search for an understanding of my gifts. Since I was experiencing connections with the spirits of loved ones of friends and acquaintances, I felt that the spiritualist church would probably be the best place to start.

I looked for books to find as much information as I could related to all that I was experiencing or had been experiencing. I didn't know anyone else like me or anyone who was familiar with anyone like me. Back then, people never really talked about such things because it was thought they were crazy or weird.

I believe I have always been on my spiritual journey in one way or the other. Only now I feel I am more aware of my journey and what my life path is all about. If you have read my book *Take Charge*, it will make more sense as to what I mean about being more aware of my life and my life's journey.

As you become more aware of who you are and what you are about, it becomes clearer what you want in life, what we want for ourselves, what we want to do, and what path to take. It is important to self-examine, to go deep within and really do some soul searching to find yourself.

The important thing is once you find out who you are, accept yourself for who you are. If there is something you do not like about yourself, ask yourself why you don't and what you can do to change and to like yourself more. That is what we call personal growth. Be open to improving yourself, open to growth, to be a better person. Once you are happy with who you are—including all your faults or quirks— you gain self-confidence. When you have self-confidence, no one can bring you down.

Awareness

Was I always aware of this path? As mentioned earlier, I have probably been on this path but just not aware of it. Since childhood I felt I had a calling to help people. I have always felt compassion towards others. Growing up I witnessed my parents helping those in need of help. They were always generous to those in need.

Even though we were not well to do, my parents were always willing to provide meals or a place to stay in our small home. No matter who they were, everyone was treated like family. I believe such a way of living is a spiritual way of life.

Since this was considered a way of living, or the only way of life I knew, I recall thinking as early as 8 years old, *I like this. I love what my parents do for people, and I would like to do the same when I grow up. I want to be caring, helpful, and generous towards others.*

All my siblings are kind, caring, and generous towards others. I call it our family thing. I feel proud and happy to say that I have such a family who is kind and generous. Since this was our way of living and being unaware of anything different as my parents were very protective and seldom allowed us to be exposed to outside life, I did not know that the world outside our family was very different.

After my marriage was arranged, I was in a different life setting. I began to see that the bigger world was so different. I could not understand why people were greedy, selfish, cruel, and materialistic. I saw all of this in the family into which I was married. Family members fought with each other over money. Such behaviour was something that did not exist in my family.

This new world was quite a shock to the sheltered life I grew up in. Being in an emotionally and verbally abusive marriage led to situational depression and unhappiness, and I needed to find a solution to the problems I faced. In an effort to understand how to get myself out of the challenges I faced and overcoming my fears, I dove deep into learning more about myself. During those times, I was certainly not aware of my path. I was too busy surviving the circumstances I was living in.

I think my life challenges and circumstances were preparing me to learn more about myself, my strengths, my weaknesses, and what I wanted out of my life. Since I spent a lot of time deep inside me to find me, I became more aware of the gifts and spiritual experiences I was having. Some were even lifesaving experiences.

After having gone through so many spiritual experiences, it became impossible to ignore the phenomenon I experienced which led to questioning it. I was curious and wanted to understand what was happening. And thus, began the quest to research everything I could about my gifts, my experiences. However, I always considered myself very fortunate and blessed that I am being helped and watched over by God.

I spent many years learning more about spirituality and spiritualism. Working with the gifts I was born with helped me to understand spirituality better, and now I can say I am aware of my path and have accepted and chosen to be on it.

Spirituality

When did I first learn about spirituality? If I were to recollect how the whole idea of spirituality came about, I would say it was after I left my married life and began my journey into another world away from my family and the family I married into.

I started to see a world that was filled with people living a lifestyle foreign to me. I began to realize that there was so much cruelty and selfishness in the world. It was not something that existed just in the far distance or only in a fictitious story.

The first time I encountered the word "spiritual" was from my neighbour when I was about 31 years old. It stuck in my head, and that eventually led me slowly and gradually to learning more about spirituality. I think I started to learn more about spirituality in my early forties, and I continue to learn about it and put the pieces of the spirituality puzzle together.

I learnt more about spirituality in connection to spirit when I stumbled up on a website about spirit connections. I got hooked on watching the group chats on such sites and learnt a lot about connecting with spirits and spiritual healings. There were some mediums giving messages in reading rooms, and I found it very intriguing how accurate the mediums were about what they were picking up for the sitter.

In time, I went into the reading practice room and watched beginners practice their abilities. And soon I was one of the beginners who got a connection and gave information that was coming through in what seemed like a movie in my head. The amazing thing was the accuracy of the details that I was getting was incredible. The first time that I did a reading was for over two hours.

It was many of these similar experiences that motivated me to learn more about spirituality so I could use my spiritual gifts to help others. I continue to learn about spirituality every day and how the universe is leading me on this journey.

I also learnt to trust that all things will be well so long as I have faith and trust in God to know that I will be guided to do what I am meant to do if I listen to my inner guidance or my inner voice, what some may call intuition. If you listen to your intuition, you can save yourself a lot of aggravation caused by getting yourself in harmful situations.

Sometimes our inner voices can be a guide coming from our guardian angels watching over us. We all have guardian angels with us who are looking out for us. If we only reach out or within, we can hear the guidance we need. That is why we often hear the phrase, "The answers are within ourselves. All we need to do is dive within."

Spiritual Experiences

It was the various experiences I encountered which led me to understand that I had experiencing some unusual phenomena considered to be spiritual experiences. At the time, being a logical person, I had difficulty understanding what all these experiences were, and I tried to make sense of all these occurrences. Fortunately, none of these strange occurrences did not scare me or get me concerned. I just simply shrugged them off as I was more focused in dealing with overcoming life challenges.

Unusual circumstances and situations will start to occur and lead you to your spiritual gift(s) one way or the other, whether we want to or not, or if we like to or not. If we are truly meant to be working with our spiritual gifts to serve humanity, and if we are taking a turtle's pace to go on this journey, the universe has a way of creating circumstances until we pay attention.

Yes, unusual phenomena occurred so I would have no choice but to pay attention. Examples of such occurrences were that my stereo would suddenly turn on while I was watching television. After repeated attempts to turn off the stereo, it continued to turn on by itself. Then I finally pulled the plug out of the socket. My car engine would start running on its own while parked in my driveway while I was in the house. Passers-by would knock on my door to inform me that my car was running and the car locked.

When I go into my memory bank, I can pull out many spiritual experiences that remain crystal clear to this day. I shall share with you the ones I feel were so helpful in my life or were practically lifesaving events.

I recall clearly one Sunday I was on my way to work. Snow was coming down heavily, and I had a fair distance to get to work. In clear weather or clear traffic, it was an hour's drive to work. Since I did not have a specific start time to get to work, time did not matter.

With heavy snow, all the cars were moving slowly, at twenty kilometres an hour. Most drivers were keeping a fair distance apart. Then suddenly, a car ahead of me in the lane towards my right took a spin and about to do a 360-degree turn. I was right in position to be hit, and possibly get into a fatal crash.

I saw no option for me to miss the crash, be it stopping since I was already going at twenty kilometres, and to speed up to get out of range was also risky. Then I heard an inner voice tell me, "Do not worry. Carry on just as you are." Fortunately, I felt calm and kept driving as I was. The car in front of me took another funny spin and missed me entirely. It crashed into two cars behind me and another car in the left lane behind me. I have to admit it was certainly a sign that I was well protected.

When I was living in Vancouver, British Columbia, I had just left my marriage and was going through a rough patch in my life, with its struggles and challenges, I felt depressed and ready to throw in the towel. I lay in bed feeling rather sad, unable to see the light at the end of the tunnel.

I started to pray for help to get through this struggle. Suddenly I felt I was picked up from where I was lying and held in an embrace. I was shown a vision in which I had climbed a steep mountain and was almost at the top. I was directed to look down to see how far I had already climbed, and it would be a shame to let go. I was advised to rest briefly before I continued to climb, but I must just hold on and hang in.

Once I understood that it would be a shame to give up after all the efforts I had put into climbing such a steep mountain and did not have too far to go, I felt I was placed back down on the bed where I lay.

Another incident was when I was visiting Whistler, British Columbia. I had gone to Vancouver to seek a second opinion about a major surgery that was recommended to me by my specialist. I had registered at a Holiday Inn for an overnight stay.

The room I was given was on the seventeenth floor. When I entered the room, it seemed like Fort Knox. It had three security bolts and a chain lock on the door with a sign hanging that read, "Please lock your room." The room was just big enough to fit a bed. There was no room for a night table, so there was a table by the foot of the bed. The window had iron bars on the outside, so it would be difficult for anyone to climb in and out of the room.

After getting ready for bed, I set out my medications and water on the table, although I was concerned about reaching for it when I woke from pain. I always placed my medications and water by my bedside table so I could access them during the night when I awoke from extreme pain.

After settling into bed, I fell asleep only to be woken up in excruciating pain. The inability to move made it difficult to reach the table for my medications. In desperation, I started to pray for some help. Soon after, I felt a pair of hands start to massage my neck and shoulder. I reached my hand over to my neck and felt a pair of hands. For a moment I was frightened. Then I started to wonder, *Who, could come into my room?* Then I remembered about all the security locks and the iron bars outside the windows. There simply was no way anyone could possibly get into the room.

With the comfort of knowing that no humans could possibly get in, I just allowed myself to be comforted by whoever's hands were helping my pain. Soon after I fell asleep and woke up pain-free. And I remained pain-free for days.

I feel very fortunate to have had so many beautiful spiritual experiences. I know I am always watched over and protected.

Links

As I mentioned previously, I didn't realize I had spiritual gifts because I did not think too much of the unusual experiences I had. And a lot of them I shrugged off as my imagination. I practiced mediumship reading online, and even though I did it quite accurately, I still didn't think too much about it. To me, it was something I did to entertain myself.

The moment that made me take notice to the fact that I had a gift of connecting with spirits was when I was performing reiki on a client and felt a link to the client's mother. She had given me a message and showed me a vision of what message she wished me to give to her daughter lying on my table.

I was surprised to have had such an imagination as I had wondered, *Why would I? How could I have imagined about her mother? Did I in fact feel the presence of her mother, who actually wants me to give her a message?*

Being sceptical of what I thought could even be possible, I asked my client about her mother and where she lived. She replied, "My mom is dead. Why do you ask?"

I was taken aback and did not know how to respond to that as I had never been in that position before. How do I tell her that I think her mother has a message for her? I made an excuse for inquiring about her mother. However, my client was persistent with her need to know why I asked and eventually, in my defence, I blurted out everything I saw and felt what her mother had said. To my surprise, my client told me she knew why she got that message and explained the vision I saw and the reason for it.

Other incidents occurred when I would do healing on someone. I would get a link to their loved ones, and the messages were sometimes in a language I did not know only to find out the intended recipient understood the message. Some would be brought to tears of joy from such unexpected messages from the spirits of their loved ones.

As these incidents occurred more frequently and having confirmations that they were not my vivid imagination, I realized that I did indeed have a gift. With these confirmations, I started to pay attention to my other experiences and began to realize that I have other gifts.

I learnt about my gifts as an empath, why I always felt what I felt around people, why I was able to feel people's thoughts, emotions, and pains. Over time, as I learnt more about myself, I learnt more about my gifts, including the gift of healing. Now I mentor people with such gifts to be empowered, to manage their gifts, and to use them to help others.

When I was in my mid-twenties and married at the time, I had felt my father's pain when he was having attacks of pain while on his flight to Canada with my mom and my two siblings. On my sister's pleading, the captain turned the flight back to Karachi.

That very night I had dreamt that my father had passed, and I made all the necessary funeral arrangements. I thought it to be odd as I am the youngest of eight children. Although it didn't make sense at the time, I had a knowing that I could not ignore this dream. So, I decided to fly out and bring my family back home to Canada with me. On returning, I had a very strong feeling and a knowing that my father did not have long to live and that he had cancer. Since he was not yet diagnosed, my husband said I was crazy, and asked me how I knew that. I told him, "I do not know. I just know. And why I know I don't know, but I feel certain of it."

Not long after my parents and two siblings migrated, my feelings and dreams became realities. Despite numerous confirmations of events revolving around my gifts, I was still sceptical and shrugged them off. I was not willing to realize my gifts because I was too logical and liked to make sense of everything. I still do like to analyse everything to death.

As I started to use my healing gifts, my spiritual gifts developed and grew stronger and stronger. It made it impossible for me to ignore my gifts, and I learnt to accept them, even though I couldn't find logical explanations to my experiences.

I admit that I am at the point in my life where I am not all that eager to find explanations for everything I experience nowadays. I feel comfortable and confident with the gifts I have and know I am being divinely guided to do what I am meant to do. I have the comfort of knowing that my acceptance of, rather than fighting against, my gifts has helped me tremendously.

Chapter 7

Life with Spiritual Gifts

My Gifts

I have already told you what gifts I am blessed to have. Now I will go over the information in a different way to ensure that you have a clear perspective of my gifts. Being an INFJ empath, I have the gift to sense people's physical and emotional pains. I can sometimes feel their thoughts and can at times be a human lie detector. I have the ability to sense and feel all of these even from a distance, especially of those with whom I have a close bond. In those cases, I am able to know who I am feeling. However, I do have difficulty knowing whose feelings I am picking up on if I do not know the person well.

My gift as an empath can be related to the gift of clairsentient, another name for clear sensing. From what I am aware of, with this gift I can not only sense a feeling of something, I can also smell the presence of someone passed who may try to make their presence known.

I have even been able to smell things from a distance. This is freaky when I am able to smell the aroma of the food over a TV channel as if I were in the kitchen where the food was being cooked. I have the gift to sense, feel, and see passed spirits in my mind's eye. I saw a spirit with my physical eye once and will never forget this experience.

I am able to receive a link from the spirits of a loved one of someone I know or who is around me who may want me to give a message. I feel their energy and feel what the spirit wishes to relay. Sometimes the spirit may show me a vision in my mind's eye.

I do not know how to call anyone from the spirit realm. Nor do I know who will come to connect. Therefore, if anyone comes to me with the hope that I can connect to a specific loved one, I cannot promise to do so. However, I will wait and allow myself to be open to any link that may come through.

I do not know if other mediums have the ability to call on anyone, but there are plenty of people out there who take advantage of vulnerable and grieving individuals by pretending they can. This saddens me because it creates a bad reputation for genuinely gifted individuals.

I have also been blessed with the gift of healing. This is something I learnt after I endured multiple health issues which led me to seek alternative healing since traditional medicine was of no help. After experiencing positive results with alternative healing, I decided to practice such healing and help people like me who suffered from so many health issues. I started a healing practice with the intention to heal people from their physical pains. But I soon realized my gifts to heal emotional pain were more prominent. So over time, it has come to feel as if I am being led to help heal the emotional pain.

I have the gift to teach or impart knowledge to others. I feel that I somehow intuitively know how a person absorbs information and find myself teaching individuals in ways they are best able to learn. I do not have a set method to teach everyone.

I have the gift to speak different languages; I am multilingual. I learned to speak multiple languages with ease.

I have the gift of creativity. I like the creative arts. I love to be creative, and I get lost in my creations. My mind feels like an endless source of creative inspiration. I am told my brain never stops.

Realization

My gifts emerged from my early years. And since I was still at an early stage of my life, all experiences were new. I did not have any comparisons to make. Nor did I have much contact with the world outside of family. My parents never said anything was different about the dreams I had, though they did pay attention to them when I shared with them.

The only time my mom would say to me, "It's only a dream," was when I woke up in tears, afraid of my dream coming true. I had seen in my dream one of my siblings being hurt by friends. I did not know at the time that seeing prophetic dreams was a gift that not everyone experiences. I thought it was normal for most people to have this type of dream.

When I felt my heart skip a beat and felt a knowing that my brother was in a car accident and having it confirmed hours later, or when I had known with certainty that my father had cancer even before he was diagnosed, as well as similar incidents, I still did not realize that I had a gift. I just thought I had the ability to feel things and know things, but I did not question it.

My gifts got stronger, and unusual incidents started to occur more frequently. When I started to have more exposure to the outside world and capable of feeling my surroundings, not knowing why and how I could feel things and know what I knew became overwhelming and difficult for me. I started to struggle with it.

When I started to experience connection with spirits—and after realizing I was not imagining them—I searched for information about my experiences. Gradually, more and more information started to come my way. Sometimes I was led to the information I needed to find to learn more about myself and my gifts. It did take me some time to grasp the notion that I have gifts as I was made fun of and labelled as someone crazy or weird. Fortunately, by then I was comfortable being who I was, and such remarks did not affect me enough to keep me from learning about myself and my gifts. I must admit understanding these gifts was quite a journey.

Advantages

I am sure you can easily guess some of the advantages of my gifts. However, I am happy to share with you my perspective on the advantages I feel by having these gifts. Before I understood my gifts, you may be able to understand that they felt like double-edged swords. Earlier on, I did not feel the advantages of having such gifts.

There were many occasions when I honestly wished I did not feel what I felt, and I did not want to know how or why. It was difficult to comprehend and accept because I saw the disadvantages of my gifts, and how they made me feel. I think back about being overwhelmed by all the energy I absorbed. I felt discomfort on a regular basis. I felt anxious, agitated, and irritated. I was often on edge and impatient. Since I saw and felt these disadvantages, I did not want to feel all the energy I was absorbing from my surroundings.

Over the years, after learning more about myself and my gifts and having a better understanding of my experiences due to my gifts, I learnt to manage and live with them. To some degree, I was able not to let experiences overwhelm me. It helped me to feel much calmer than I often felt in the past. I am now able to say I do feel there are many advantages to my gifts. If I go back in time to when I thought having gifts was a disadvantage, I can now relate the advantages to my premonitions, dreams, and intuition.

In regard to my dream and feelings about my father's funeral and illness, at the time it felt like a disadvantage. No one wants to know or feel that a loved one does not have much time left. I dreaded the thought of losing my father and wished every day for this feeling to go away and for it not to happen.

Even though I did not feel the advantage of this knowledge, I did take advantage of this knowing as, against my husband's wishes, I made efforts to spend more time with my father daily. I did not care if my husband got angry with me for spending some time with my father after work. I knew I wanted to spend as much time as I could because my feelings were strong and definite. It was more important to me than facing my husband's anger when I got home.

As an empath, I can feel people's physical discomforts, and I have the advantage of feeling their relief while I practice healing on them. Another advantage is the ability to sense and know when someone is lying to me, although there are still times when, due to my trusting nature, I can miss that. The ability to sense and feel some people's thoughts have their advantages, too, because it helps me understand people who have difficulties expressing themselves.

I get a knowing or intuitive feeling about certain routes to avoid when I leave home. Advantages to avoid being delayed.

The advantage of the ability to speak in multiple languages helps break the ice when meeting new people from different countries and cultures. It helps people feel comfortable communicating with me and feel at ease around me.

People tend to gravitate towards me when in need of help. They are comfortable sharing their innermost stories which allows me the opportunity to help them deeper with my gift of healing.

Disadvantages

Before I understood my gifts and the advantages of what they had in my life, I considered them disadvantages because it was not easy living with such gifts. Having these gifts is not as much fun as perceived. The main disadvantages are the burdens I feel at times of what I feel. The physical as well as the emotional pain we all know is difficult to live with.

It is hard enough to have to go through such pain when you have a reason for your suffering. It is harder to experience all these pains because I am absorbing pain from people around me. Worst of all is that I do not only pick up or absorb the pain of one person; I am able to absorb pain from more than one person at a time, and that can compound the pain I experience.

Another disadvantage is when I feel someone is lying to me, pretending to be a good friend. Meanwhile, the person's intentions and motives are purely selfish. Such situations sadden me. I feel at a loss and cannot understand how people can be so deceitful and are comfortable being so.

Sensing and feeling people have no time restrictions. So, without warning, I can feel or sense something about someone at any time. Quite often I have difficulty sleeping because I wake up in the middle of the night feeling someone's pain or knowing a potential problem surrounding an individual.

The spirit of people's loved ones can just simply step in any time to give a message. This can be draining if they unexpectedly show up and hang around for an extended time. Sometimes I feel I do not have the freedom to rest because I am bombarded with too many energies coming at me. Although I have learnt to manage my gifts quite well, I am prone to feeling overwhelmed on occasion, and I do not know what it's like to have a good, restful sleep

No matter how well I may be able to separate myself or my feelings from those I absorb from others, it is impossible to isolate myself completely. It is still possible to penetrate through me though I have the skills to protect my energies. Knowing how to protect myself from the unfavourable effects of my gifts has certainly helped me tremendously so that I am now able to focus on using these gifts to help myself and others around me.

Acceptance

I do not have any control over who and when I sense a feeling. I cannot choose whose energy I can or cannot absorb. Before I understood my gifts and was picking up on a lot of energies or emotions from people, I was not quite aware of whose emotions I was picking up because I was too engrossed in what I was feeling and why. Now that I understand I can feel people's pain and emotions, rather than wondering why I was feeling what I felt, I try to sense whose energies I am feeling or picking up on.

I also do not or am not able to choose the geographical locations where the energies I am picking up on. I can at times feel something may be happening with someone I know who may be in a different city or state, but it is very random.

I just never know when or how I will have information on future events, whether it be in a dream or just a feeling of knowing. I cannot choose to know what I want to know. That is why I never give anyone the impression that I can predict on demand. I do allow myself to sense and feel and pay close attention to what I sense and feel about a certain thing a person may request.

If I am fortunate to sense something, I will share it. If not, I cannot pretend to feel and make up stories. I cannot call on an any spirits of loved ones as per anyone's request, nor am able to tap into anyone's energy if they have their protective energy barrier that they are not aware of.

Even though I may receive a spiritual link, I am not always able to obtain the name of the person who is linked to me. I can relay the information provided, but for unknown reasons, I do not get their name. I have only been able to get names on a few occasions. I generally feel the presence of the spirits as opposed to seeing them. I have seen a spirit through my physical eyes just once. I do not know why I was only able to see that time and not other times. That is why I say I accept and work with my gifts as they are.

Way of Life

For those of you who view having a gift as an advantage, you may think it must be so cool to have such a gift. You may assume that if I want to know anything about future events, I can. Or that I can make random predictions on demand, or even predict a winning number or which stocks will do well in the market. I have been asked these questions many times in the past.

I don't make any attempts to predict anything with the stock market. Nor do I want to because I feel strongly that I cannot or must not use such gifts for financial or material gains. I feel I am to use these gifts to bring love and light to people around me or who are in need.

You may already have some idea from what I have shared about the advantages and disadvantages of my life with gifts. I do not know how others live with the gifts I possess or how they manage them. But I can relate to those who are still understanding the gifts they possess and the unusual experiences they go through. After all, I went through them myself.

Now that I have learnt how to accept and manage my gifts, I mentor those who are going through these phases in their lives through my healing journey program, which I started eighteen years ago by chance. Unbeknownst to me when I started practicing reiki, it would lead me to mentor people learning to live with such gifts. I feel I was guided to do so. I had no idea at the time how this healing journey program was going to bring about amazingly positive changes in people's lives and in the lives of those around them. I have witnessed their personal growth in self-confidence and strength.

I feel blessed to live with these gifts because I know that I can really help people. I have always felt it was my calling to help others, ever since I was a child and watched my parents help others.

I remember very clearly how much I admired my parents for what they did for others. I must have been 7 years old when I thought, *I love how my parents help people. I want to be like them when I grow up.*

Knowing how much good I can do with my gifts, going through the challenges I experience from it is worthwhile. It is not easy going through the difficulties I experience, especially when I am absorbing a multitude of physical and emotional pain from others and endure many sleepless nights as a result. I feel I am always telling myself that everything is fine. Meanwhile, I am struggling on the inside, trying to separate what is not mine and concentrating to detach the feelings of others from me.

I feel these gifts have taught me to live my life consciously, to be aware of how I live, how I treat others, and to consciously choose to be the person I am. I choose to be kind and helpful. I choose consciously not to let people's negative treatment change me but continue to be kind and loving. I believe love is the most powerful healing energy. For me, it is important to maintain this loving energy in my heart.

Love conquers, love forgives, love thrives, love is light, love will lead the way. I am confident in the power of love.

Chapter 8

Life as an Empath

My Life

Now that you have a good understanding of what it is like for me living with my gifts, you must be wondering what more I could I tell you. Right? As you have read earlier, the INFJ personality is rare. Being an INFJ empath puts me in a rarer category.

Being in an extremely rare category—only .05 per cent in the world's population—it is not easy to meet others like myself. I also fall into the category of multipotentialite empath and a few other empath categories.

As an INFJ, I tend to feel many things intuitively. As an ENTP, I tend to live in my head. You can imagine how conflicting this can be to have these two traits which are completely opposite from each other.

I feel fortunate to have the combination of thinking and feeling traits because it gives me strength in both which delivers balance in my life. I am fortunate because when I am making any important decisions, I weigh it out by both logic and feeling, head and heart.

When they are both in agreement, I make my decisions. When I do this, I find the decisions are the right ones for me.

Being a multipotentialite empath, I have an interest in so many things and always a thirst to learn everything I am interested in. I expect myself to be good in everything. Sometimes I am even interested in learning things that are useful and beneficial, whether I like them or not.

I have this strong need to excel in everything I do. I am not sure if it is the INFJ or the multipotentialite part of me. Whatever it is, having this strong sense to excel in what I do can be difficult as I tend to be hard on myself. And since I know I am hard on myself, I set high expectations of myself.

I struggle at times to understand why people do not care enough to put effort into what they do. I am often told I am my own worst enemy because I am hard on myself or expect too much of myself, as well as that I spend too much time in my head and drive myself crazy because I must analyse everything to death.

Having a combination of INFJ and multipotentialite makes me a very creative person, so I feel fortunate because my mind is always in creative mode. I can't help but want to get my hands into something creative, be it handicrafts, arts, or writing.

Once I get creative ideas, I feel I must see if I can materialize them. When I do, it is very rewarding. However, the downside is that if I get the idea in the middle of the night, I don't have the patience to wait and see if I am capable of doing so or not, so I can have sleepless nights because of that, aside from sensing other people's energies.

Having a creative interest has been very helpful for me. When I went through a rough period in my life, I found it to be therapeutic. I found it comforting to be lost in my creative zone as it helped me heal from some of the painful years of my marriage.

I often sought comfort in being creative. It gave me a break from the constant suffering I endured in life. I guess that is the biggest advantage and supersedes any disadvantages my gifts might bring. Being lost in my creativity was very comforting and healing for me at the most painful period of my life, and I feel very fortunate that it was what saved me and my life.

Struggles

You already know now that empaths absorb all kinds of energies and how overwhelming that can be. In my teenage years, I did not hear or know about empaths. I was in the dark about being an empath.

I had always suffered severe headaches or felt sick when I went out shopping with my siblings. My mother would prevent me from shopping with my sisters because she told me that I was always sick after having gone out. Now when I think of it, it must have been that I had absorbed too many people's energies. I find it difficult to be in big gatherings because I feel drained if I spend too much time with too many people. That is tough because I have a large family, and when our family gets together, I need to find a quiet corner to spend time even though I do not mean to be antisocial. If I stay in a crowd for too long, I feel the urge to leave sooner than I should or actually prefer.

When I feel others' pain, it makes me feel sad. It is hard for me to snap out of at times, even when I am consciously aware that I am feeling someone's sorrow, which is frustrating. At times I so wish that I could easily wave it away when I know I am feeling something that is not mine. If only it was that simple, I wouldn't have to struggle with it.

When I sense people lying to me or deceiving me, I sometimes struggle to let the person know that I know they are not being honest. I tend to see how long people think they can fool me. And INFJs are famous for our door slams. We will tolerate it till we reach our limits, and then we shut the door. That's what I do. But I struggle prior to making the decision to do the door slam. Once I shut the door on someone, it's final.

Since empaths are sensitive to other people's emotions, I sometimes find myself going over things in my head for a fair length of time, especially if I need to say something to someone.

I struggle with the information I receive about people. The struggle is worse if it's not positive information. When I am not sure if I know how it will be received, I sometimes end up repeatedly running over in my head till I find a solution to how I should share it.

It can be a struggle when someone is expecting me to help them with my gifts, and I feel bad when I cannot promise to be a definite help. I can try, but there is no guarantee. I feel a burden when I can feel their expectations of me and don't know if I can meet them.

On many occasions I am asked, "Can you tell me what you can sense of this person or that person?" What people do not understand is that empaths may have the ability to sense and feel people's emotions and pains and sometimes even thoughts, but there are times when a person is very closed off. That can put up a barrier for me to sense anything.

It's also possible to be unable to read another person because there is a protective barrier around that person's subconscious. It can be difficult or hard to penetrate.

Empowered Empath

When I first realized that I am an empath, things started to make sense to me. I learned why I felt what I felt and why I experienced so many things and did not know why. I didn't even know there was a name for it. It took me almost half my lifetime to stumble on this name for the type of person I am, or even my personality type. Perhaps I came on it earlier but was not ready to take in the information. I am not sure. It is quite possible I may have, but since I was too busy putting the pieces of my life together, there was simply no room for me to take in anything else.

My spiritual awareness became prominent when I was at a point in my life when I was soul searching or even self-searching. Then other pieces of the puzzle started to fall into place.

I was free from concentrating on overcoming challenges, so now it was time to understand the spiritual side of me. When I was able to relate to the information about empaths, what I had experienced and why, I researched on a regular basis about the pros and cons of being an empath and how to put up a protective shield to prevent myself from absorbing too much around me. I researched how to restore my energies by being close to nature and water and how the body of water is very good for cleansing the energies that I may have picked up from others. I learnt to close my spiritual points as protection.

By understanding and accepting these gifts and how to use them to my benefit, as well as to help others, I feel empowered because I dwell more on the positives and the advantages of being an empath.

By learning how to manage my gifts and how to protect myself, I now help others to do the same. I have worked on raising the vibration of my energy and am now helping others to raise their energy vibrations as well by filling our lives with the energy of love.

Energy of love is the most powerful energy and is at a higher vibration. The energy of love has the power to heal and to defuse anger or any other negative emotions. The energy of love cultivates kindness, harmony, and peace.

Becoming an empowered empath has taught me to plant seeds of love within my heart and encourage others to do the same. The more seeds of love we plant the more loving energies are around us. The energy of love is light. Where there is light there is no room for darkness to reside. Where there is love, anger or hatred cannot reside. I try to mentor those who just realize they are empaths and are struggling with their gifts to grow and become empowered by learning to accept their gifts and how they can use their gifts to spread love and light to all they meet. It's like being a lighthouse for the sailors in dark, stormy nights.

I feel that it is our responsibility as empaths to assist others to see the light, to appreciate goodness, how to look for the good in people, and to help others cultivate their inner goodness.

I think like many things in life, I am sure, over time I will learn more about being an empath. After all, there is no set manual that comes with us when we are born. We learn every day as we go about our lives. When I learn more down the road, I will surely share it in my future books.

Do Struggles Continue?

Becoming an empowered empath has certainly helped with understanding the reasons I struggled so much with pains and emotions that did not belong to me. Learning to reduce the absorptions of energies around helped me a great deal. I no longer cried for no reason or had any other symptoms I picked up from other people.

As much as I have learnt to protect myself, there is no guarantee that it is fool proof protection. There is a good likelihood that I may still have the possibility of picking up energies of others. The ones I feel I will most likely pick up first are those that I am close to.

I still wake up in the middle of the night, feeling someone's fever and nausea at the same time the person is experiencing them. I feel exhausted and tired due to the energies I pick up of people I have a close connection with.

I woke up in the middle of the night and was prompted to turn on the television to watch the news because it was important. The moment I turned it on, I got the news of a brush fire in California that was heading towards my sister's home. I was frantic and called to check if they were OK. I had not been aware of this fire since I had not watched the news or television for a few days.

There are times when I feel I do not want to know certain things because I just don't want to know. Perhaps because I may not want to deal with something. Knowing means I may have to find a solution to what I feel. If I am tired, I may just not want to have to deal with it. But due to my personality trait, I don't rest until I have a solution to everything that needs one.

The struggle continues because as I have accepted my gifts and used them to help others through my healing work, my gifts get stronger, which means I feel and sense more and more easily and more frequently. Since there is really no timetable to when and how I may absorb the energy around me, I could be taken by surprise by what I pick up or absorb.

INFJs are very self-critical individuals. I feel that I must excel in everything that I do. On a positive note, it is a good thing because I put my heart and soul into everything I do or am responsible for. But on the other hand, I can't help questioning if it is good enough. Have I given it my best effort? Even though I have, being so self-critical means I lean towards wondering if I have really given my best efforts. This is how I am hard on myself. This is one struggle I have yet to overcome.

I am driven and committed. If I have a project at hand or if there is a question that needs an answer—and at times there may not be a simple solution or even an answer to the question—I won't give up till I find a solution and answer, no matter how long it takes. This can be quite consuming because I refuse to believe that sometimes things are just the way they are.

I would then have to learn new ways to manage and hone my gifts. Or perhaps take more time for myself should I need it. I feel no matter how much I learn to manage them the struggles continue. But to what degree I don't know. It is something I will learn more as I travel along my path.

Managing My Gifts

There are various ways for empaths to manage their gifts. I am sure there are many empaths who have found their own ways or methods to manage their gifts. Some of them have shared what has worked for them.

The most common method many empaths have shared is to use meditation. When someone mentions meditation, you and many others most likely would have the image of sitting quietly, eyes closed, palms up, legs crossed. That is something I just cannot do because I am too active to sit still like that. Do I meditate? Yes. But I found my own way to meditate. To meditate is really to focus one's mind and be rid of mind chatter. I meditate by walking in nature. Or I could be doing something active and repetitive.

Water is the best source for me to clear energies that are not mine. When I feel overwhelmed with energies, that is my first choice. I may simply soak in the bath for a while. This is one method that is good especially during winter, when it is too cold to go to a body of water such as a lake.

Nature and water are good remedies for me to use to manage my gifts. I made the decision to move out of the city and am now residing close to nature and the lake. Making this move has helped me tremendously. People have noticed the difference this move has made on me, even commenting on the fact that "It's the best thing you have done for yourself. You seem happier." What they did not know was what I was living with before my move and the impact the gifts had on me daily. In fact, I think I didn't even realize how much it had affected me. After moving close to a lake, it was so convenient for me to just walk to the lake every time I was feeling out of sorts from absorbing too much. However, there are times when that is not enough. When that happens, I reach out to my friend for healing and to help me feel more like myself again.

Grounding is also a good way to help myself, and I like to do that by walking barefoot or working in the garden. I cannot say I am an avid gardener, but I do like to do some. Crafting for me can be very meditative, and I can get into a meditative zone and replenish myself. Working with flowers is also very therapeutic for me. I find myself rejuvenated when I sing and work simultaneously.

I believe there is no single method for people like me to manage our gifts. Since each of us is unique, our personalities and our paths are unique. We can learn through trial and error what will work for us. We can certainly try the different methods that are recommended, and through our experiences, we will find what works the best. I may recommend several ways to manage, but ultimately, it's up to each individual to learn for himself or herself what works best.

Chapter 9

Responsibility

Lightworkers

You are probably wondering what I mean by the responsibility of the gifted. Or you may already have some understanding that with such gifts comes a price. I feel our Creator created everyone to be unique, so everyone has a different purpose in life.

Some of us are created for specific purposes. We are known to be the lightworkers; our purpose is to shine light to those in need.

I can't say for sure that there are responsibilities attached to the gifts we are born with. I feel that I have some responsibility or should be responsible. I feel that I should use the gifts I have responsibly. I also feel that the gifts should be used for the benefit of others instead of for myself, and especially not for material gains for myself or for people I encounter. You must be wondering, *What, good is it then if I cannot use it to help myself or those I know for financial gain? How is it of any help?*

I feel the gifts can be used for benefits in many other ways which are far more valuable than any financial or material gains.

I can use my gift of healing to help people heal on so many levels—physically, emotionally, and mentally. When we are healthy as a whole, we can feel happier and more at peace within, which I think is far more valuable than any monetary or material gains. When we are happier and at peace, it is easier to build yourself up financially. It will feel less of a struggle.

Using the gifts, I have to help in healing is not all that simple because even if I make a commitment to help someone, this does not mean I can really make it happen. The person seeking my help must commit to helping himself or herself.

They must want to help themselves enough to make a commitment to the work the healing journey requires. After all, I am not able to simply wave a magic wand and make it happen overnight.

Time and dedication are needed from both parties for the healing journey to be successful. If I spend all the time and energy trying to help but the other person does not put in the effort to grow and bring about positive changes in their life, then all the time and effort I put into helping would be fruitless.

On some occasions I have felt people expect to leave all the responsibility on me to make their troubles magically disappear. What I do feel responsible for is to help and guide others to acquire the tools necessary to help themselves. Then they can grow to be confident and strong enough to endure any life adversity and find love and peace within themselves rather than search outside themselves.

It's like the phrase, "Teach them how to fish rather than fish for them." I admit that sometimes I feel that because I am so determined to help people. I somehow feel responsible to help everyone who crosses my path and tend not to give up on those who are not willing to put in the effort to work on helping themselves. I had to learn to accept that I am not responsible for everyone who needs help. I had to accept the fact that I am allowed to be responsible for helping those who seek my help and give my full commitment in doing so.

Helping Others

"Why be responsible?" I get asked. I am also asked, "Why do you feel that you are responsible to help everyone or fix people's problems?" Well, that is a question I ask myself too. I really do not have an answer. I just feel an innate urge that I have to do something when I see someone in need.

I have been like this ever since I can remember, an urge that is so strong I feel I must do something to help make things better for someone. When someone seeks my help, I feel responsible to see through my promise to help, and I do not give up until I see the results of having made a difference.

I also feel that perhaps I was blessed with my gift for the very reason to help others, and I am responsible to make sure that I do in fact put all my effort into making the most of the gifts I am blessed with. I feel I am on this path to be of service to others, spread love and kindness, and am responsible for planting seeds of love wherever I go and with whomever I meet.

I do not know how other gifted people like me feel. I have not had the opportunity to share this conversation because I have only met people who are just becoming aware of their gifts, are trying to understand it, and are learning how to live with them.

I also relate to the phrase, "Great gifts come with great responsibilities."

Jacinta Yang

Being Responsible

What is it like to be responsible? In all honesty, this is a bit too tough to give a clear-cut answer. It is not as if someone made me feel responsible for anything or anyone. Feeling responsible is something I feel that is inborn in me. I can't help but feel it. It is because of the responsibility that I feel motivated to do what I do with my life.

I think it's great to feel responsible. It provides a purpose in life that I must follow. I live my life with a purpose and am responsible for my actions no matter what I do. Therefore, it is important for me to use my gifts responsibly.

There is a downside to feeling responsible for others even though it is not asked of me. Feeling the responsibility can also at times be difficult because it can cause me some sleepless nights or restless days. My brain is constantly churning, trying to find solutions to problems. My determined character will not let me rest until I find a solution because I believe there is a solution to every problem. So I must find it no matter what.

Being responsible also means to follow through on anything I put my mind to do or who I help to the very end. There is simply no giving up on anything with me. I tend to be hard on myself, and to give up on anything or anyone feels like failure to me. And you and I both know it is not a pleasant feeling to feel like a failure.

I tend to be hard on myself, and I have high expectations of myself as well. Therefore, to allow myself to be defeated by any problem is not an option I will allow myself. So, feeling responsible to seeing something through can be challenging.

It is a good thing that I actually like challenges because I thrive on them. If I didn't, it would certainly be difficult to feel responsible.

The Burden

I am sure you can relate to the idea of the burden of being responsible. We both know that if we are responsible for something or someone, it is up to us to ensure that everything goes well with what or who we are responsible for.

At a job, when we are responsible for a project, it is up to us to see it through from beginning to end. We have to come up with a plan to carry out the project as well as find solutions to any problems that arise. We must ensure that we complete the project with the best result in a timely fashion.

As parents, we have the responsibility to care for our children. We are responsible for their needs while they are young, and we are responsible to raise them well.

What do I mean by the burden of the responsibility relating to having gifts? It is that while I feel responsible to help, the inability to help at times feels burdensome. I also feel responsible to be sure that my actions do not harm or hurt anyone else. Therefore, it is important for me to be aware of my actions at all times. That means I cannot be careless in my words and actions. I also feel that I should always be available to those in need. However, this is sometimes not possible.

Aside from our actions, our thoughts have the possibility of affecting others energetically. It is important, therefore, that we do not have negative or angry thoughts towards others. It is important that we be responsible, kind, and loving no matter what so we do not fester in anger.

As human beings, we are prone to all kinds of emotions that arise from situations we encounter. I have learnt that if we keep love in our hearts, it is possible for us to diffuse the anger that may be caused by people or situations. When we are able to do that, then we won't feel the burden of being careful about our thoughts and actions that may be hurtful or harmful to anyone.

Can I Carry This Responsibility?

I am by nature a responsible person. It seems like second nature for me to just take on responsibilities without being asked. To answer the question, "Can I carry this responsibility?" I do not doubt it for one moment. I know that whatever responsibility I may need to carry due to my gifts, I will find a way to do so.

I feel that being on my path with these blessed gifts, my responsibilities shift from time to time as I am guided along the way. Hence the responsibilities come with duties that I am to fulfil on my journey. When I started on this journey of providing healing energy, I was healing on the physical level. Then it shifted to healing on the emotional and mental well-being levels. Now it leans towards the spiritual as the responsibility of helping others spiritually is being layered on. I feel my gifts are growing stronger in areas where my responsibility lies. Circumstances and events seem to lead to what I must do or how I must apply my help.

It pleases me to know that the efforts I am making towards helping people are making differences in their lives. It makes me happy to know when I receive their confirmations and feedback. It is this feedback on how my efforts are positively changing lives that encourages me to carry this responsibility of what I am here to do with my life on earth.

Chapter 10

The Healing Journey

What Is It?

I have endured multiple health challenges and suffered from excruciating and chronic pain—although some of it may not have been mine—due to undiagnosed medical conditions. I had numerous surgeries. After my last surgery, I was termed high risk for surgeries and was put on regular treatment for nearly twenty years.

While going through these health challenges, I tried every alternative treatment available to me: reflexology, chiropractic, massage, Chinese herbs, acupuncture, and reiki. I am aware that alternative healing does take time as it helps with the root cause. But I could not afford these services as they were not covered by health benefits. Being unable to work made it difficult for me to pay for the full treatments, so I chose the shorter treatment option. The results made me feel the same after the session as how I felt before the session.

I stumbled upon reiki and started going once a week. Eventually I noticed that my regular monthly hospital visits to the emergency diminished. It was then I decided I would learn more about this healing modality and become a practitioner. I took a course in reflexology since I always had an interest in the foot as well as knew that the foot holds the map of our body, and we can find relief by working on certain reflexes in the foot.

Reiki was something I felt, and it led me to my spiritual awareness. I felt practicing reiki heightened my gifts, and I started to sense and see more. I was able to connect to the spirit realm while I channelled healing energies.

When I practiced reiki on my co-worker, I experienced a vision of her past life. At the time she was going through a difficult phase in her life. I felt the intuitive need to recommend regular reiki sessions, and during these sessions, I was able to see visions and receive messages from her spirit guides.

Since all these experiences were very new to me, I felt I should recommend that she start journaling everything that was coming through. I suggested that she make notes of any experiences she felt and of any messages she got with each session. That was when I felt that I should call these regular sessions as the healing journey and see where it would lead her.

Over time, I began to notice a difference in her, although at the time I could not quite put my finger on it. She seemed more at peace and calmer, focused, to name a few. I asked her if she noticed anything different about herself. She told me her family had noticed a positive difference in her.

She recommended that her sister come for healing sessions, and it went from there. I began to feel it was something I should do. When people came to me seeking relief with their health issues, I have occasionally felt I was guided by healing guides. Being an empath, I can feel the discomfort of my clients and as I work on the areas, they feel the discomfort and relieve their discomfort. I too become relieved. I practiced alternative healing part time as I worked as a freelance floral designer along with going through my own healing journey of the medical conditions I suffered.

When I decided to practice holistic healing, I decided that I was going to work on clients by a session rate rather than an hourly rate. I wanted to be able to help clients feel a difference when they got off the table.

Once the news of my ability to bring forth a message during reiki sessions got around, people sought me for my reiki service solely for the purpose of a possibility that I may be able to connect to their loved ones. Even though I would express to them I did not have the skill to call on anyone to come through, clients still wanted to try my service for just a chance of a connection coming through.

Fortunately, most of the time I did receive a link and was able to give messages. Over time, I realized that there was a different kind of healing evolving.

Why Does It Help?

When I was channelling messages for my clients on the treatment table, it helped them to heal emotionally. I began to feel the ability to provide them guidance in what they needed, and I soon noticed the difference. And as I did with the first client, I decided to call the healing sessions the healing journey.

I felt the urge to recommend they start to journal since they would come for regular sessions as they began to feel the benefits of the sessions. I felt I was being guided along the way to help my clients to help them become comfortable with themselves.

I noticed the sessions, in the way I practice reiki healing, the messages that I channelled helped clients become stronger and more confident as individuals. I also noticed that they felt calmer, and anger started to dissipate over time.

When I saw the differences, I was able to bring about in people's lives, I felt that I should offer the healing journey services as it was helping them emotionally as well as physically. Soon it became apparent to me that my gift was to help people heal mentally and emotionally.

My holistic healing, which started out to help people with chronic pain, seemed to have taken me on a different path. I still help clients with physical pain, and they do feel the benefit from my sessions to be more effective than those from other practitioners they have been to.

It has now led me not only to help clients with emotional healing but with their spiritual growth. I just know I am being divinely guided as I am merely a channel for healing, and I listen to my intuition as how to help my clients.

I feel the healing journey service that I started to provide my clients has been helping them tremendously. So, I feel that it is my calling. I shall share stories of a client's journey that she wrote and wishes to contribute to this book so others may benefit from her story.

Journaling

I eventually realized I am a conscious channel. I often do not recollect what I channel, and people would often tell me that "Oh, by the way, the things you told me have come to fruition," or, "What you said is going to happen is happening now." I have no recollection of what

I may have said because I most likely channelled it because I do not even remember having such a conversation.

Because I would not remember the conversations I channelled and messages were coming through when I did healing sessions, I felt it would be best for clients to journal the information and the changes they experienced. I felt intuitively that doing so helps them with the progress they are making in their healing. It helps them to stay motivated to continue to work on their progress in healing and reach their goals of feeling confident, strong, and happy.

I also felt that revisiting the journal helps the healing to continue. The energies of the healing received at the time of the entry is made would still carry the healing energy. When someone rereads the entry, not only will the individual see how far they have come in the healing journey, the healing energy can still be felt from the entry.

I believe that when clients journal their healing journeys, they become more aware of the transformation that has taken and is taking place in their lives. Where they were and where they have reached.

Revisiting the Journal

Another reason recommended journaling when I began offering the healing journey service, was because I felt it was important to not only document how they felt prior to the session but what they experienced during and what they continued to experience days after the sessions. They should also note when the changes occurred and to help them pay attention to how they feel as some changes are subtle.

By paying close attention, clients learn to go within more and become attentive to their inner selves, leading to learning to listen to inner guidance. Journaling everything that occurs helps them to remember the changes that have occurred for them. When they see where they are at the time, they revisit their journals, it helps them by encouraging clients to know they have done an amazing job of helping themselves in their personal growth.

Writing and revisiting the journal helps individuals decide how much more they want to work on their growth. It also helps them to see and understand what else they might want to achieve for their futures. It helps them find themselves and to be who they want to be. They are helped to discover what they need for inner peace and what would make them happy and to achieve it. It teaches them that self-love and self-acceptance are the keys to joy and happiness.

Understanding Personal Growth

From my observations, I saw that many have learned that life is never without challenges. When we begin our lives and go through life experiences, our lives are affected by people and situations every day. The challenges that we face can have a strong impact in our lives. As I have mentioned earlier, experiences can make you bitter or better. People and challenges can cause emotional strain in our lives. If we allow the situations to consume us, they can destroy us and make us bitter. Holding on to bitterness robs you of inner peace and happiness. When you decide that you do not want to be a victim of life circumstances and wishes, you make changes in your life so you can be happy. That is the first step in understanding what you want for your happiness.

The next step is to heal from the pain you have endured from what you lived through. You then find your step to grow to understand yourself. The more you go within yourself, the more you understand about your personal growth. And when you understand what you need to do for your personal growth, you are able to learn how to deal with life challenges without letting them destroy you.

Understanding personal growth helps you to become stronger and be confident in yourself. When you are comfortable being who you are and accepting and loving yourself, you will not allow anyone to destroy your inner peace and happiness.

Transformation

When you decide to heal your life and yourself, you go through the process of healing and journaling which helps you see for yourself the shift you have made and the efforts you have made to grow to help yourself. Revisiting your journal encourages you to continue to grow because you see the changes and growth that have happened since you started working on healing your life.

When you see the improvement and changes, you are encouraged to carry on your journey to help yourself grow and not feel like a victim. When you continue to grow as a person, you transform your life.

You are able to see for yourself the transformation from the person you were when you first decided to heal yourself and your life. I have been told by my clients that they feel that they have come out of a dark hole into the beautiful bright light.

I liked to share a story with you that was written by a client who was kind enough to share the story of her healing journey. She has given me permission to use her full name as she feels that by doing so, you will know she is someone real and exists.

Her name is Anne-Marie Henzel. This is her story in her own words. The events are extracted from her healing journey journal.

Jacinta Yang

Anne-Marie's Healing Journey

When a person reaches a state when they believe a thing must happen because they do not wish it, and that what they wish can never be ... this is really the state called desperation.

This was my state of mind when I first began my healing journey. For me the healing journey was a last desperate attempt to regain some semblance of sanity and balance in my life. I had reached a brick wall and felt sad and trapped every single day. I could not sleep at night and took no joy in the aspects of my daily life.

I heard of Jacinta but was somewhat hesitant, and yes, even nervous, to go for a session. Finally, I decided to give it a chance because I felt that at that point, I had nothing else to lose. I recall the first time that I met Jacinta before my session. She was kind, gentle, and very welcoming, which put me at ease right from the beginning.

She explained in detail everything that may or may not occur during the session, which helped to alleviate any apprehension that I had. Not long into the session, I felt calm and relaxed.

Three times I heard muffled voices in one ear that were very distinct in sound but too garbled to understand clearly. This, I later discovered, was my first introduction to my spirit guide. I heard the voice and felt the presence, but could not actually see him ... though that has changed over time.

I left the session feeling very relaxed and with the first stirrings of hope that I had in several years. This was when I began to set aside some alone time each evening to meditate and to be alone with my thoughts.

Being alone with your thoughts can sometimes take you to dark places that you may not wish to face ... and so it did! This became the time of my acceptance of the issues in my life and my decision to follow through on this new path in order to face my issues, understand them, and deal with them.

My next session opened the doors to inner peace for me, as Jacinta began to explain to me and guide me through the benefits of truly looking at your inner self. Not the person that goes about interacting with people, and social situations, but rather the person *inside* ... the one that only *you* are acquainted with.

This became a phase, where slowly, I began to realize in many cases I was the cause of many of my problems. I forced myself to be brutally honest with myself, only to discover that in essence, there were often times when I allowed myself to be my own worst enemy.

I began to work on myself and to take a long hard look at what was wrong with *me*, rather than automatically seeing myself as a victim. This was a time that brought me the most profound changes in my life.

I used to cry every single day! Then I would cry once or twice a week, until slowly, and with Jacinta's guidance, I was able to replace those tears into words ... first in my journal and in my poetry, and later to communicate with the person who was the cause of my depression.

It was difficult at first as I am not a person who enjoys confronting others ... let alone speaking my mind. It was, and is, something that I am still working on, but it is not the fearful experience today, that it was in the beginning.

The issues with my family members have improved greatly as I no longer allow myself to be drawn into the negative thoughts and actions that once used to define my entire life and, in turn, my happiness and peace of mind. This has been a time of personal discovery.

This time of personal discovery was also the reason that I continued my sessions with Jacinta. As I opened myself more and more to the wonders of what my life *could* be, I became more open during my sessions. I always said a prayer before each session for God to guide Jacinta into my newly opened mind, and to surround me with the white light of His Holy Spirit.

At some point during my next session, a bright white light appeared behind my closed eyes. This light pulsed and waned, and continued throughout the entire session. It was a very dark and rainy day, and at first I thought that the sun had come out. I opened my eyes to see, but the room was still dark, and the rain was still falling. Then I realized that this light was actually brighter than the sun and very different in its luminosity.

When the session was over, Jacinta told me that this was only the second time that she had ever seen what she witnessed during my session. She saw winged angels all around me … everywhere! I felt happy, but I was not surprised. I *knew* that something very special and unique had occurred during this session.

Jacinta told me that eventually, these angels would make themselves visible to me. And later … they did! This was only my third session, but it was the first time that I experienced a visible and tangible "something", and I knew that it was an experience that I would never forget.

It was also the first time that I came to the realization that I am never really alone. I know that I am being watched over. I sense it … I feel it … but most of all, I *know* it! Around this point in time, I began to journal. Jacinta said that it was important, though at the time, I didn't really see the point in it. However, I also knew that Jacinta had never led me astray, so I trusted her instincts and began to journal.

I told myself, "I will never forget any of these things … I don't need to write them down to remember." But I did forget! Very gradually, the details of my sessions began to recede in their detail, and the chronology of the events began to get lost. From this point on, I kept a journal and now realize the importance of it. When I revisit my journal, I find that there are many things that have slipped my mind … many of them are things that I do not ever want to forget. My journal seems to keep me grounded and helps me to stay on track … always moving forward. Often it serves to remind me when I am regressing.

Sometimes, I read it from the very beginning, and I am filled with an overwhelming sense of wonder at just how far I have come. I believe that it is not fully possible to achieve full transformation until you are able to understand the full extent of your personal growth.

I have experienced things that I never would have believed possible had I not physically been an integral part of it. I have felt the treatment bed vibrate underneath me. I have seen angels and have been raised up upon their long robes. I have experienced astral projection and have spiritually travelled to the Hall of Records, and much, much more. "Euphoric" is the one and only word that can describe my experiences over the last four years. It took time, belief, trust, and dedication to reach this point, but I would not trade the benefits of my journey for any other human experience that exists.

I could write a book detailing my many discoveries about myself during my sessions, but my story is only one of many. Therefore, I have condensed it in order to cover the most crucial things that have changed my life the most. In doing so, I hope that I am, in some small way, extending a hand or a message of hope to others who find themselves in a situation similar to my own at the beginning of my journey.

When I look back and read about the sad and desperate woman, I was four years ago, I feel a true sense of gratitude for the people and the path who led me to this new and wonderful liberation of mind, body, and soul. I feel those same emotions towards Jacinta but must add that I am grateful for the patience she has with me.

I have been a difficult client at times, who constantly needed to be guided through situations that I was certain I could never handle on my own. She alone has proven me wrong more than once, always being there for me when I doubted my own strength. I was so happy when I found out that Jacinta was writing a second book. And I feel honoured and proud to have had this opportunity to share my own story within the pages of what I feel is more than a book! It's a new way of living and a true path to self-enlightenment (8 September 2020).

Charlotte's Experience

I have been praying for miracles for the healing of my mother's dementia and my father-in-law's lifelong anxiety, depression, insomnia, and dizziness. Plus, I've been wanting to develop my psychic abilities, but I didn't know how, and I got a message that I would meet a lady guide who would help me.

Then I was introduced to Jacinta about three weeks ago by two friends whose children were being mentored by Jacinta for their spiritual advancement. Jacinta was able to tell me quite a lot about me, my daughter, and my mother just by looking at me. I knew that she was the answer to my prayers! I bought her first book immediately and got her contact information.

My husband and I met her two days later, and we each received reiki healing from her, and then, just by looking at us, she was able to tell us a lot more about my children, my mother, and my father-in-law's health issues stemming from his difficult childhood. We were really impressed and asked Jacinta to do distance healing for my mother and my father-in-law.

Jacinta then set up crystal grids for them in her home and sent distance healing to each of them. My father-in-law then enjoyed the best sleep, in years in the following weeks and was happy and energetic! He was willing and able to go fishing with my husband, take walks with his wife each morning right after breakfast, practise ballroom dancing at home with his wife, read storybooks, and even play his old favourite music CDs at home, which he had not done in many years! We were all amazed and super happy for him!

I brought my daughter and sister to Jacinta's house, and we each picked out some crystals. Jacinta taught us about the different crystals and how to open and close our chakras to protect ourselves, as we are empaths and are easily affected by others' energies. The crystals I bought from Jacinta have been giving me pain relief, stress relief, and healing every day! I am forever thankful to Jacinta for her wonderful reiki sessions and healing tips!

When I met Jacinta, I was going through a very stressful time with some difficult people at work, and I had many sleepless nights. Jacinta gave me reiki sessions to calm and relax me. She also taught me to sleep with purple amethyst crystals so that I was able to calm down and sleep well. She also taught me to keep a lilac crystal on me to help me communicate better with difficult people at work, which really helped!

My sister later had a recurring bladder blockage and could not pee for hours; she had to go to hospital emergency to get a catheter inserted to drain her pee. I texted Jacinta to ask her to send distance healing to my sister ASAP.

Jacinta called me immediately and asked me to give my sister my red crystal beads to place on her tummy/bladder area, so I did. My sister said she felt immediate pain relief as soon as she placed my red crystals on her tummy/bladder area. Whenever she took the red crystals off, her bladder pain would return and become unbearable very quickly until she placed the red crystals back on her tummy/bladder area again.

Jacinta also set up a crystal grid for my sister and sent her distance healing that night. The next day I drove my sister to see Jacinta for a reiki session, and a day later my sister was able to pee on her own and got her catheter removed!

I also brought my sceptical teenage son to see Jacinta for a reiki session. After that my son became much more open with the rest of our family and was willing to spend time to talk and joke around with us and play board games with us, instead of always hiding and playing computer games in his bedroom at home. We were pleasantly surprised with his change of attitude!

Jacinta sensed that my daughter was meant to write healing stories for others and kept encouraging her to write. It was true that my daughter has been a gifted writer since grade 2. Jacinta then read some of my daughter's writings and exclaimed that my daughter had actually channelled some of the stories which have deep healing messages for humanity from the divine! Jacinta is kind and encouraging and is an excellent spiritual coach for my daughter, my sister, and me!

My daughter started getting her period for the first time about three months ago (at age 11), and kept getting her period every two weeks after that. It was painful and annoying for my daughter. Jacinta gave my daughter reiki sessions, and my daughter's periods have become normal and monthly instead of bimonthly.

With Jacinta's teachings, my daughter and I made crystal water to drink, and my period went down to four days from seven to ten days within a month. My daughter's period went down to five days every four to five weeks and was very light, from seven heavy days every two weeks before that. Thank you very much for your wonderful healings and teachings.

Jacinta also gave my stepdaughter reiki healing and helped her destress and reenergize her body and mind so that she could focus on meeting her tight work deadlines. My stepdaughter has also gladly accepted Jacinta as her spiritual coach.

I have asked Jacinta to set up a healing grid next for my brother and my father when she can. We have faith in Jacinta that she can and will continue to do wonders with her healing power for everyone in my family! We have seen so many positive changes in just the short three weeks since meeting Jacinta! We highly recommend Jacinta for healing and spiritual coaching/mentoring (30 September 2020).

Chapter 11

How I See Life

In Conclusion I like to share an excerpt from my book *Take Charge* on how I see life.

How I See Life

Compiling of views of life in different ways: The meaning of life has always been a big topic for me. Having had the life I had, I have always felt a need to express my pain and experiences to find comfort for my soul.

My habit of expressing myself was always through analogies, and I found it so much easier to do so this way. Expressing myself metaphorically is also another method that makes it so much easier to make sense of what is within me that needs to be formulated outward.

Over the years, I have written material about life, which includes poetry, and I would like to share this here to conclude my book.

Life Is Like a Painting

How do our lives have an effect on others? Our lives are all intertwined.

When we are born into this world, our lives are like a blank slate or a blank canvas.

Once we enter into this life, we start to paint a picture, little by little, and details are put onto the canvas. Sometimes while painting (as we go on with our lives), we may accidently lose the balance of our hands, and we may ruin a bit of the picture—we lost our strokes, and the fine details were lost or smudged. In order to correct the accidental mistakes, we sometimes have to have patience and wait for the paint to dry so that we can paint over it. The colors, when applied over other colors, create a distinct new color. Therefore, in life, when we go through experiences, it's like the colors of a pallet: When we make mistakes and repaint with new details, it gives us a new distinctive outlook in life, in comparison to when we don't make an error in our paintings.

We can either be so inspired to paint over our mistakes and create a beautiful masterpiece, or we can simply get irritated and think that the mess in the painting cannot be repainted into a new masterpiece (which is like having no hope). We then either choose to throw out the painting (giving up), or we simply keep painting over it without giving proper care and attention, because one thinks that no matter what one does, the ugliness of the painting is going to show through, and it will.

However, when one views the smudged part of the painting carefully, the artist will be able to see how, by careful choice of colors, he can create a new, beautiful masterpiece. Making careful choices in life makes us who we are.

Life is a painting. People are the colors, and the smudges and accidents are the mistakes we make and the experiences we have in our lives. When certain colors are combined together, they create a certain distinct color. This means that people in our lives, of different personalities and characters, can influence our personality, just as society or the social setting surrounding us influences who we are.

Just like a color, no matter how we mix them, we are still able to know the base color. No matter how much others may influence us, we are still who we really are. If you don't mix too many other colors, then the base color is generally prevalent.

When we don't allow others to influence our basic principles of who we are, then we are always able to shine our true colors. Life is just as complex as a painting, with so many details and so many variations of colors.

If we choose to paint a beautiful picture, we will have a beautiful picture. When we paint with passion and interest in creating a beautiful picture or painting, that's what we will have. Therefore, we choose how we want our life to be, by being conscious of how we live it, and of the choices we make, despite experiences and setbacks.

When we are painting a masterpiece that we have a vision of, we must be sure to do the work ourselves; we cannot allow anyone else to get involved in the painting, unless it is someone who has the same vision as ourselves of how we want to create the masterpiece. If someone who does not have the same vision gets involved, or if we allow them to have their hand in the painting, the outcome will not be what we originally had hoped or planned for.

Therefore, we must decide how to handle our own lives. If we allow negative people to affect us negatively and to influence our happiness, then we are responsible for our own happiness. Hence, the painting may not be beautiful. However, if we don't allow others to affect us negatively, and we carry on with our own positive mindset, then we will be able to create our own future as we plan or want—a positive one.

We can allow others to give us advice and suggestions as to how to use colors or ideas, and then we can use our own vision to see if those suggestions will help us create what we want. If we allow ourselves to be open to suggestions and advice as to how we can handle and cope with our situations, some may be helpful and some may not. We are the only ones that will know what will help us grow and improve to be a better person, and what will not.

Although sometimes we may not be quite so aware of how to paint a beautiful picture, that's why we need good teachers to teach us. A good teacher will always be one that will try to teach and bring out the best in their students, and to teach them to create their own unique masterpiece.

Hence, having the right teacher is important and crucial to paint a beautiful picture or a painting.

Experience Life to the Fullest

When someone says, "Experience life to the fullest," what do they usually mean to say? Or how would one generally interpret it? In my observation of the general public or people I have encountered, I have come to the assumption that the phrase, "Experience life to the fullest," or, "Live life to the fullest," would generally mean for a person to experience life in the way that person would like to, or to do what they love to do, which could be a hobby or what they want in a career, or what they always dreamed of doing in life—the list can be endless, as everyone here on earth has different desires, skills, and talents.

To give an example, some people may have a passion for music, but different people with the same passion will do different things with that passion. Therefore, to each of them, experiencing music in life will be different. For some, they will pursue music as their career; whereas for others, they would like to be able to attend as many concerts as possible because of their love of music, but they do not have or possess the skill to play music.

Everyone has multiple interests and passions in life, so they would strive to achieve as many of these interests as possible in order for them to consider having experienced life to the fullest. Fulfilling one's bucket list may be what one may consider as experiencing life to the fullest.

What does *experiencing life* to the fullest really mean?

When we first enter this world, we never know what to expect, as we do not know what or who we will encounter in our lives. From the time we are born, we start experiencing life, but we are not even aware that we are experiencing life.

We are born with different senses through which we experience life. Predominantly, we are born with 5 senses: smell, sight, hearing, taste, and touch. Therefore, we experience all these five senses, and they are a part of living or being alive—hence, a part of life.

Every day, people are experiencing life, yet they are not fully aware of their experiences, as many take life for granted, going through life unaware of what life really is. Many go through it, not knowing what life is all about, and they carry on with their lives, fulfilling the expectations of others, or just fulfilling day-to-day expectations.

Some people go through life without many challenges, and they have a tendency to take life for granted until they are faced with a life threatening experience, or given news that they have an illness and that their life is now suddenly shortened. Such incidences tend to awaken many people, and they start to view life differently. Those who have taken life for granted, generally will start to appreciate life more after having a close call.

Then there are also others who have always been dealt challenges in life, and they resent the life they have; they cannot handle the challenges because of how the experiences of these challenges feel—they are too hard to handle. They then have the tendency to either end their life because they do not want to experience what their life has dealt them, or they choose to get into self-destructive behavior and get into addictions to numb the feelings of their experiences. They end up losing themselves, and they lose the desire to experience life. There are of course various reasons for this course of action that people take. For some, they may not possess an inner strength; and for some, they need support to help them deal with such challenges; and yet for some others, there may be some neurological deficiency to help them cope with life issues.

Sadly, for some people who are in such a situation and are not aware of their need for help for support in dealing with life, they are not so lucky to experience life to the fullest. Hence, they may either end up becoming an addict, trying to numb themselves, or committing suicide. Sometimes some of the people, if they get lucky and get the support they need to deal with life issues and challenges, may still have the possibility to experience life a bit more than they would have. Some could even have their life turned around, and they could learn to appreciate life and then set out to try to experience life fully.

There are also those who may have the very same challenges but accept all the experiences the challenges provide, who are also born with some inner strength, so they learn to be strong and to appreciate every experience that life offers. These are people who I believe actually experience life to the fullest, because they appreciate every experience of life. Life is filled with challenges and wonderful experiences. These are the people who understand that because they can experience some sadness, they know how to appreciate happiness. They can appreciate comfort because they know what challenges feel like. So, this is to say that one can experience life to the fullest when one is aware of all the good and bad experiences that life offers, and they can make the most of it. They accept the challenges gracefully and face them, and they still appreciate the experiences that the challenges teach them. They are grateful for the good things that life offers them. These are the people who truly are willing to experience life to the fullest.

Life and Love

Life is a four-letter word, yet when we are to describe what it means to us, there is an endless way to do so. What is life? What do we want to do with our lives? What do we want to achieve in life?

L. Living
I. In
F. Focus
E. Everyday

L. Longing
I. Incessantly
F. For
E. Everything

L. Listening
I. Intensely
F. For
E. Exquisite Music

We can go on and on about what it means to us individually, according to where we are at spiritually. We always hear the saying that life is too short, and therefore we must make the most of what we have. When we say that life is short, we are referring to this physical life that we are living. But spiritually, souls live on. The life of a soul is not a short one, but I think we should still make the most of it.

When I say "make the most of it," I mean that we must try to do the best we can to do good in all our physical lives, in order to grow spiritually.

Then there is also the discussion about *karma*. It has been said that how we live our physical life somehow affects our next physical life. It is said that if we don't do good deeds in one physical lifetime, then we may pay the consequences in the next lifetime.

However, I think that if we do our best and be loving and kind to our fellow man, be of service and help those that need us, be ready to forgive those that hurt us, and continue to love those in need of love, then chances are that we won't even have to worry about karma.

Some may say that we are just humans, and that it's not possible for us to be good and loving all the time. There may be some truth to it because as humans, we do have all kinds of emotions, and therefore we may experience love, anger, hatred, disappointments, etc. However, I feel that if we fill our hearts with love, it leaves very little room for negative emotions; and even if we may experience this, it cannot stay long in our hearts, as there simply is no room for it because it's already filled with love, and it's the overflow that rids it of any negativity that may try to enter, as it leaves with the overflow.

Love

Love is also a four-letter word, just like life, and different people have different perceptions of love.

Different people feel love differently. Some may feel love for others but only if their needs are met by others, be it material or physical. Then there is that spiritual love, where we are love, and we love all those around us unconditionally. We love them because they are also a spiritual being in a physical body, just like ourselves.

We may not like them for their actions, yet we still love them for who they are, with all their faults. They may be unkind to us and hurt us, yet we are ready to forgive them and be there for them when they need us. Because we are filled with so much love and want to be of service to others, it does not matter what they may have done to hurt us, as love in our hearts erases the hurts and injustice inflicted upon us.

Love is a powerful energy. It has been said that love heals all wounds. It usually refers to emotional wounds.

Reiki, Qi qong, and all other energy healing modalities are considered to be the energy of love. These energy healing modalities are known for helping different ailments, from the physical to the emotional. Ailments, although they may be physical, are sometimes manifested due to our emotions, caused by the daily stress of life.

Hence, the energy of love is considered powerful; so much so that it helps relieve us of the many ailments that we may experience.

The power of love also acts like a magnet, as it draws in goodness in people, and brings people, family, and friends together. As we all know, hatred has a tendency to pull people apart.

If love is the basic principle of our lives, then there is harmony amongst us. Love is light; hence, where there is light, darkness cannot exist. The two cannot cohabit. Therefore, if we choose light, there is love; and thus, there is no hatred or darkness.

When we practice love, we raise our vibrations so high that we can ascend to a fifth dimensional plane, where love flows naturally, we feel lighter, and negativity does not bring us down as easily as it would when we are in three dimensional planes.

Life Is a Journey

Life is a journey; when we first start, we do not know what our destinations are, but we do know or are aware of what options are available to us. When we first embark on our journeys, we are first learning about the different destinations ahead of us, just as a child learning to walk or talk, etc.

When we first start, our journeys are easy. As a child may have no responsibilities, life for a child may be generally easier. As we get older and become more aware of our surroundings and responsibilities, this is when we are faced with different choices of destinations. For some, the path to their destination may not be a smooth one; for others, it is a breeze. Different people choose different modes of transportation and where they want to go.

How a person's journey is going to be will likely depend on the destination they choose. However, we must keep in mind that the weather conditions can also have an impact on our journey, no matter what mode of transportation we may choose to take.

Some people may feel at a loss as to what their destination is, so they go on a quest in search of their destination, which for many leads them to a spiritual path, and on a spiritual journey. When our soul advances, we tend to take the spiritual route, which is more on a higher plane. Meanwhile, there are those that still need to learn lessons on this earth plane, so their journey will be different.

Destiny

People seem to have this notion that our destiny is carved in stone from the time we enter into this world. It is of the assumption that God writes our destiny. Why do you think people like to say that God writes our destiny? People have a tendency to shove responsibilities in their lives on to someone else other than themselves; it's better to blame God who created us.

If things do not go the way they hope, they blame it on someone else, because it's easy to, and it also frees them from being responsible for their own actions.

In reality, we write our own destiny. God created us and gave us free will to choose the life we want. He gave us free will to choose between good and bad, so how is it God's fault when things go the way they do? The outcome of our lives is based on the choices and decisions we make.

When we make decisions and act upon them without giving much thought to the consequences of our actions, we must hold ourselves accountable for the outcomes in our lives. We are the ones who create our destiny. As human beings, we are not perfect; we can make mistakes, so we can learn from them. If we accept the responsibilities of our mistakes, there is a good chance that we can learn a lesson from them, and we can make improvements.

One belief that I have in life is to have no regrets. When making any decision, think carefully of all possible outcomes from the decisions made. If the result of the outcome is not something that we had hoped for, or is not right for us at the time, it is best not to regret it or blame yourself for making a bad decision. Blaming oneself will not help one's growth, but rather it could stunt one's own growth because they would be wallowing in self-pity and not move on.

Drive to Destination of Life

You are the driver in the vehicle of life, and you need full control of your steering wheel in order to drive to the destination you choose for your life. Taking on passengers is your choice. A journey with a passenger in your vehicle will have a variable outcome.

Sometimes a passenger may only travel a short distance, and it can be a pleasant journey. Sometimes it may not be all that pleasant, but fortunately, the journey was a short one. Sometimes you may have started with the intention of going to the same destination, but you soon realize that your personality does not click, and your journey starts to become a bit uncomfortable or unpleasant. The passenger may prove to be immature or unstable; so much so that the passenger may interfere with the steering wheel, causing the ride to be bumpy or to even potentially lead to a serious life threatening accident.

It's up to you to choose to make a quick stop and let the passenger get out of the vehicle, to prevent heading to a potential disaster, or you can carry on your trip and tolerate such behavior, and face the consequences of a potential fatal disaster.

Moving forward in your journey as you resume your trip, it is best not to go over it in your head about the journey you just had with the passenger that you just dropped off, or to be consumed by the drama that was created. All these distractions that you carry in your head can also lead to a disaster, which will then set you back, and you will need time to recover and heal before you can carry on with your journey.

It is important to concentrate on the road ahead, as hard as it may be. Continue on, with a new focus on the road map with which you have planned ahead towards your destination.

When you pay attention to the road that will lead to the destination you wish to reach, you will get there for sure.

However, during your journey, the road may not always be smooth and well paved, but you know that it will lead to where you want to go. Then you just have to drive carefully and patiently according to the road conditions, to get to where you planned to reach.

Along the way, you have a choice to pick up another passenger if you wish. Bad experiences in the past do not guarantee that you will continue to have bad experiences. You may even find a passenger who may go a long distance with you if you allow yourself to take that chance, which could be a fun and meaningful journey.

Or you can choose to enjoy your trip solo, in a calm and peaceful atmosphere as you wish. Ultimately, how you choose to drive to your destination is entirely your choice.

Life is all about having choices and having the courage to take chances, and having faith and hope. You decide for yourself what you want for yourself in life. Do you want your destination to be peace and happiness? Then it is your choice to map your route. The roads that you will take are the roads named love, forgiveness, sharing, caring, faith, hope, courage, and determination.

You Know You Are Blind When ...

The world is big and wide,
Filled with trees, mountains, and ocean tide.
Nature is filled with beauty of every kind,
Yet you do not see; that's when you know you are blind.

The world is filled with people of all kinds.
You cannot tell the difference, for you do not use your mind.
That's when you know you are blind.

Every day in our lives, there are people we meet,
Be it at work, at gatherings, or on the street.
Some of these we love to greet.
Some may be rude, cruel, fake, or kind.
When you cannot tell the difference, you know you are blind.

Day to day, you have someone around you, who is there,
For you and to be with you when your heart needs a mend,
And yet you say you don't have a friend.
All the while, this person has been nothing but gentle and kind,
Yet you don't really truly acknowledge it in your mind.
That's when you should know you are blind.

You think you are smart and know it all.
It's the one mistake that will make you fall.
For there are many things still to learn and understand,
But your ego stops you from learning all that you can.
All you think is how smart you are in your mind,
That's what makes you totally blind.
You like the people from whom you think you can take, take, and take.
You don't realize that someday this will be your big mistake.
All the while you think you are great, but sadly all has been fake.

When you lose people in your life that have been real and kind,
That's when you know you have been blind.

Desperately you seek someone to fill your desires and needs.
You are presented with all the red flags of the person's bad deeds.
Yet your desperate need makes you think you don't mind,
That's when you know you are blind.

You have people around that care about you all the time.
You do not see and act as if you don't give a dime.
You think all is good; things with them will always be fine.
When things fall apart, it never crossed your mind,
That's when you know you've been blind.

If you have someone whom you hold close and dear,
They will always be there to help take away tears and fears.
Always remember to keep them in mind.
Make sure, in this case, you don't be blind.

Conclusion

I feel my quest to learn about myself and dealing with my multiple health issues led me to my healing journey for my physical well-being that led to me becoming aware of and accepting my spiritual gifts. When I learnt I was blessed with spiritual and healing gifts, I felt guided to help people to go on their healing journeys.

I found that the healing journey not only helped my clients to heal physical issues but also their emotional and mental issues. It helps to bring about balance in their lives, helping them achieve confidence, strength, and peace within. I noticed, too, that it also helps them go on their own spiritual journeys.

For me, I feel that after overcoming my life and health challenges, I was able to pay attention to the spiritual gifts I had, mainly being an empath, and that led me to my spiritual journey.

Offering the healing journey services to my clients ultimately led some of them to their spiritual journeys. I feel if you allow yourself to be open to personal growth, you will always be guided by our divine Creator.

Printed in the United States
by Baker & Taylor Publisher Services